Make Your Life Worthwhile

Other Writings by
DR. EMMET FOX

MAKE
YOUR LIFE
WORTHWHILE

EMMET FOX

~~~~~~

~~~~~~

HarperSanFrancisco

A Division of HarperCollins*Publishers*

Library of Congress Cataloging in Publication Data

Fox, Emmet.
    MAKE YOUR LIFE WORTHWHILE.

    Reprint. Originally published: New York : Harper & Row, 1946.
    Includes index.
    1. New thought.   I. Title.
BF639.F672   1984   248.4'8998   83-48456
ISBN 0-06-062913-4

93 94 CW1 16 15 14 13

PREFACE

〜〜

THESE short essays speak for themselves. They are actually a series of practical instructions in successful living.

True success: happiness, peace of mind, prosperity, and real health are within the reach of all who sincerely want them, and who are willing to pay the price.

The price you pay is to read these lessons carefully, not once but several times, and then to apply them to the solving of your own practical problems both great and small, for the only way to demonstrate this teaching is to live it.

This book may be regarded as the next step beyond its predecessor, *Sparks of Truth*.

CONTENTS

ix

Make Your Life Worthwhile

WITHIN you is an inexhaustible source of power, if you can but contact it. That power can heal you, and it can inspire you by telling you what to do and how to do it. It can bring you out of the land of Egypt into the Promised Land flowing with milk and honey. It can give you peace of mind, and, above all, it can give you direct knowledge of God.

That power is Scientific Prayer.

There is no problem that prayer cannot overcome, and no good thing that it cannot bring into your life.

This is the message of the whole Bible. It was summed up by Jesus when he said, *The Kingdom of God is within you.* Man is slow to realize this, and he wastes his life running after outer things and missing the one thing that matters. He is like an impoverished farmer who has a gold mine under his fields but doesn't know it. He writes and telephones the bank frantically for credit. He pleads with relatives and with money lenders to help him— and all the time the gold mine lies under his fields untouched and unsuspected.

This truth was dramatically illustrated by an incident which happened in real life a number of years ago. The body of a tramp, clad in rags, was discovered near a lime kiln where he had evidently crept for warmth. After the autopsy his clothes were torn up to be put into the incinerator, and, sewn into the lining of the trousers was a bank note for a large amount. Unquestionably the original owner of the suit had had it sewn in there for safety, and for some unknown reason lost track of it.

Consider the situation! This poor hobo had sat down

many a time to lukewarm coffee and stale bread or pie, and was probably glad to get it—and all the time he was sitting on a thousand dollars, and didn't know it! Had he realized the wealth he possessed he would have slept under a roof on the fatal night, instead of in the fields —and so preserved his life. Perhaps he would have made a new start with that capital, and done well.

Most people are like the hobo in some respect or other, because most people feel a lack of some kind in their lives. They may have plenty of money and yet be hoboes for health or happiness or spiritual experience.

Riches do not become wealth until they are realized. A talent is dead until it is exploited. Cash your bill at the Bank of Heaven and make it productive in your life.

Behold, *now* is the accepted time; behold, *now* is the day of salvation.

LION INTO DONKEY

THE *one great enemy* of the human race *is fear*. The less fear you have, the more health and harmony you will have. The more fear you have, the more trouble of one kind or another will come into your life. The only real problem of mankind is to get rid of fear. When you really do not fear a situation it cannot hurt you. Of course, you must remember that fear often exists in the subconscious mind without your necessarily being aware of it. The best evidence that you have gotten rid of fear concerning a particular subject is a sense of joy and happiness about it.

The great thing to remember is that fear is a bluffer. Call its bluff, and it collapses.

An amusing incident happened in Holland a number of years ago. A lion escaped from a traveling circus. Not far away a good housewife was sewing near the open window of her living room. The animal suddenly sprang in, dashed by her like a flash, rushed into the hall and took refuge in the triangular cupboard under the staircase. The startled woman supposed it to be a donkey and, indignant at the muddy prints it left on her clean floor, pursued it into the dark closet among the brooms and pans, and proceeded to thrash it unmercifully with a broom. The animal shook with terror and the angry woman redoubled the force of her blows.

Then four men arrived with guns and nets and recaptured the animal. The terrified lion gave himself up quietly, only too glad to escape from that dreadful woman.

When the good woman discovered that she had been

beating a lion, she fainted away and was ill for several days.

This story illustrates perfectly the demoralizing power of fear. Our good housewife completely dominated the lion as long as she thought he was a donkey, and as long as she treated him as a donkey the lion thought she was very powerful and was in abject fear of her. When she discovered her mistake, the old race belief of fear came back and, although she was now perfectly safe, she still reacted in accordance with the race tradition.

Get rid of fear. Concentrate your fire on that, and other things will take care of themselves.

The treatment against fear is to realize (make real to yourself) the Presence of God with you and His unchanging love.

"He that feareth is not made perfect in love."*

* 1 John 4:18.

LOOSEN UP!

Loosen up. As a certain character on the air used to say, "unlax." Do not be tense. To be tense is the surest way to fail in any undertaking great or small.

To desire success is a splendid thing but to pursue success too tensely is to make certain of missing it. There is an attitude of mind which may be compared to a clenched fist, a knitted brow, and set teeth; and this attitude cannot bring success.

The carefree attitude of approach in any endeavor is a short-cut to success. In music, in sport, in study, in business life, many people fail, or advance very slowly, because *they make hard work of it.* They would succeed beyond their wildest expectations if they would treat it as fun.

Treat your work as fun. Regard the difficulties as part of the game, laugh off the annoyances, and the whole picture will change for the better, and stay changed. This, of course, is the real difference between work and play. Many men work harder playing golf than they do at any other time, but they do not know it, because to them it is a game.

Take it easy. *Loosen up!*

CAPITALIZE YOUR DISABILITY

SUCCESS consists in the overcoming of difficulties. All men and women who have made a success of any kind have done so by overcoming difficulties. Where there are no difficulties to be overcome, anybody can get the thing done, and doing so cannot be called success.

There was a time when laying a telegraph line from New York to Boston presented many difficulties. Then there was a time when doing that was easy, but laying the Atlantic cable was a great achievement, because of the difficulties which had to be overcome. Later on, marine cable laying became a routine business, but radio across the ocean presented problems which for a time were insuperable. Then those difficulties were overcome too.

There are no personal problems that cannot be overcome by quiet, persistent, spiritual treatment, and the appropriate wise activity.

If you have a personal disability that seems to keep you from success, do not accept it as such, but *capitalize it* and use it as the instrument for your success.

H. G. Wells had to give up a dull underpaid job because of ill health, so he stayed at home and wrote successful books and became a world-known author instead. Edison was stone deaf and decided that this would enable him to concentrate better on his inventions. Beethoven did his work in spite of his deafness. Theodore Roosevelt was a sickly child and was told he would have to lead a careful retired life. He was a very short-sighted and nervous little boy. Instead of accepting these suggestions, however, he worked hard to develop his body and became, as we know, a strong husky open-air man and big game hunter Gilbert wrote Pinafore on a sick bed, wracked with severe pain.

The owner of a fashionable dress business in London was the wife of a struggling clerk. He was stricken with tuberculosis. She had never been to business, and had no training of any kind, and found herself having to support a husband and two children. She started with nothing but good taste in clothes and a belief in prayer, and is a wealthy and successful woman today. She says, "I thought I would like to sell the kind of clothes I had never been able to afford to buy."

Whatever you think your disability is—*capitalize it*. Your particular problem will always seem to be especially difficult, but spiritual treatment and courageous determination can overcome anything.

Problems are sign-posts on the road to God.

KREISLER WAS ALL RIGHT!

WHAT we experience is our own concept of things. That is why no two people see quite the same world, and why, in many cases, different people see such different worlds. To put it in another way, we make our own world by the way in which we think; for we really do live in a world of our own thoughts. It follows from this that if our thinking is faulty, our conditions must be faulty too until our thinking is corrected; and that it is useless to try to improve outer things if we leave our own mentality unchanged.

Let us suppose for the sake of example that a deaf man goes to Carnegie Hall to a Kreisler recital; and that he happens to be a very foolish person. He sits in the middle of the orchestra and, of course, he does not hear a sound. He is annoyed at this, and changes his ticket for a seat in the first balcony. Here, naturally, he fares no better, and, foolishly thinking that the acoustics of the building are at fault, moves again to the top balcony. Still he cannot hear a sound; so now he goes downstairs again and this time chooses a seat in the very front of the orchestra, only a few yards from the violinist. Of course, he has no better fortune here, and so he stamps out of the theatre in a huff, declaring that evidently Kreisler cannot play, and that the hall is badly designed for music.

It is easy for us to see that the trouble is really within himself, and that he cannot remedy matters by merely changing his seat. *The only thing for him to do is to overcome his deafness* in some way, and then he will enjoy the concert. He must change himself.

This parable applies literally to all the problems of life. We see inharmony because of a spiritual lack within ourselves. As we gain greater spiritual understanding, the true Nature of Being opens up. As long as we move from one place to another in search of harmony, or try to bring it about by changing outer things, we are like the foolish man who could not hear Kreisler, and ran about all over the theatre.

THE THREE GIFTS

I N THE old fairy tales we were often told that when a little prince was born the fairies came to the christening with gifts. One is tempted to ask what gifts we would choose for ourselves if we had the ordering of such matters. In other words, what are, let us say, the three best gifts that a child could be born with?

I suggest the following three: *a good constitution, a good disposition,* and *horse sense.* I think that a child endowed with these three qualities would have very few difficulties to meet in life.

I put a good constitution first because health is the greatest of all human blessings. Without good health nothing else is of much use, and, of course, everyone realizes this.

On the other hand, people do not always realize how much difference a good disposition makes in oiling the wheels of everyday life. They do not realize that if you have a good disposition you make friends everywhere, without making any special effort in that direction. A good disposition saves you from criticism, resentment, condemnation, jealousy, and all the other negative things that spoil people's lives.

Finally, I come to plain horse sense. I believe that sheer horse sense, as it is called, is more important than the possession of any kind of mere ability or even great talents can be. It will do more to get a boy or girl through practical difficulties than all the instruction ever given. We have all known men and women of the utmost brilliance, who apparently had every gift for success in

10

life, but who, owing to a lack of simple, plain horse sense, came to shipwreck.

Now, supposing you feel that you were not endowed with one or any of these gifts, what can you do? Well, the Jesus Christ teaching tells us that no good thing for which we pray is withheld. If you want any of the above gifts for yourself, pray for it each day, by claiming it; and build it into your character by acting the part in every circumstance that arises.

"When you pray believe that you receive and you shall receive."*

* Mark 11:24.

MAN controls his own life. The Bible says that God
has given him "dominion over all things," and
this is true when he understands the Truth; and the
Truth is that your outer conditions—your environment
—are the expression of your mentality, and nothing
more. They are not cause; they are effect. They do not
come first; they follow after. You can change your
thoughts and feelings, and then the outer things will
change to correspond, and indeed there is no other way
of working. You are not happy because you are well.
You are well because you are happy. You do not have
faith because things are going well. They are going well
because you have faith. You are not depressed because
trouble has come to you, but trouble has come because
your realization of the Truth had first fallen off.

The secret of life then is to control your mental states,
for if you will do this the rest will follow. To accept
sickness, trouble, and failure as unavoidable, and perhaps
inevitable, is folly, because it is this very acceptance by
you that keeps these evils in existence. *Man is not limited
by his environment.* He creates his environment by his
beliefs and feelings. To suppose otherwise is like thinking
that the tail can wag the dog.

If you have been thinking that outer conditions are
stronger than you are, and that they can prevent you
from expressing yourself as God intended, say to yourself: *"Tail wags dog"*—and immediately reverse the belief.

God means you to be healthy, happy, and free, and

you must not accept anything less. Claim that God works through you—and believe it—and nothing can keep you back. *Who did hinder you that ye should not obey the Truth?*

ARE YOU DYNAMIC?

W HAT is a dynamic person?
Many people think they would like to be what is called dynamic but it does not appear that they always have a very clear idea of what that expression really means. Sometimes they think it means being somewhat aggressive and noisy, or even bombastic, in manner. In other cases, they seem to think it means drawing attention to themselves in some less blatant but equally effective way. In reality nothing could be farther from the truth.

A dynamic person is a person who really makes a difference in the world; who does something that really changes things or people. The magnitude of the work done may not be very great, but the fact still remains that the world is a little different because that person has lived and worked. That is a dynamic person.

Dynamic people, like St. Paul or Washington or Napoleon, change the lives and destinies of millions of people, and their work is known to all; but there are many men and women up and down the country whose works are not well known or known at all, and yet on their own scale they are dynamic, because they have actually changed the world in even a small way.

If you really get something done, no matter how small a thing it may be, you are dynamic, and the world is different because you lived in it. If you are only pretending to do things or talking about them, or building up appearances, you are not dynamic; you are play acting. You are a hollow shell, and no one wants to be that.

A DYNAMIC PERSON

ONE who does something in a new way, which is also a better way, is dynamic. One who makes two grains of wheat grow where one grew previously is dynamic. One who builds up a successful business serving the public and finding employment for others is dynamic. One who produces a useful invention is dynamic. One who composes fine music, writes great poetry, or produces fine paintings or statuary, is dynamic.

One who really heals is dynamic. One who teaches effectively is dynamic.

Now all these people leave the world at least a little different from the way in which they found it. Washington changed the course of history; and you may change one person's life by healing or teaching him, or merely inspiring him by your own demonstration. But the point is that something has been changed for the better in the outer picture.

There are foolish people who are quite satisfied with being *considered* dynamic. They are satisfied to pretend. They are satisfied to spend their energies on appearances. They assume an important manner and talk in a large way—necessarily somewhat vaguely—about the wonderful things they are doing or have done at some remote time and place. They are adept at giving big names to small things, and, of course, all this is but an elaborate form of bluff, and is the opposite of being dynamic.

The real secret of a dynamic personality is to *believe that God works through you*, whatever you may be doing; to put His service first, and to be as sincere, practical, and efficient as you know how. If you will put this method in practice for even a short time you will be surprised at the remarkable results that you will obtain, and you will find yourself becoming a truly dynamic person.

To give real service is to be really alive.

"By their fruits ye shall know them."*

* Matthew 7:20.

ARE YOU FOOLING YOURSELF?

THE Jesus Christ teaching is a dynamic gospel. It really changes things. It makes the life history of the individual utterly different from what it would have been without it—and naturally that is the test. Those who do not understand our teaching sometimes say that we fool ourselves; that we pretend to be healthy when we are sick, and pretend that things are going well when in fact they are going wrong. They think we are Pollyannas, trying to hypnotize ourselves by calling black white.

Of course, this is quite untrue. Anyone who acts in that way is not practising the Jesus Christ teaching. We understand that by turning away from the negative picture to positive Truth, and holding to that Truth in consciousness, we heal the picture. And that is the case, and that is the test.

That is the test. If the outer picture changes you are working rightly. You are not fooling yourself or just indulging in emotional dissipation. If the outer picture does not change in a reasonable time, you are fooling yourself. You are not working rightly, and should revise your method. The outer change may be incomplete or even comparatively small as yet, but as long as *the outer picture is changing*, you are not fooling yourself; you are getting results.

There are no invisible demonstrations. You demonstrate your mentality at all times in the outer world of appearances. Excuses, prevarications, any kind of self-deception are idle when we know that the outer picture tells the tale, and that there is no appeal from it.

17

Thank God for this wonderful Truth, for it gives you an infallible method of overcoming limitation and error.

"By their fruits ye shall know them."*

* Matthew 7:20.

18

FORESIGHT AND HINDSIGHT

Wʜᴇɴ you have to make a decision or take a certain action, all that you can do is to do the best you know *at that time*, and if you do that you will have done your duty. In the light of after events it may turn out that you made a mistake, but that will not be your fault because you could not possibly do better than the best you knew *at the time*. The wisest man that ever lived could do no more.

For this reason it is very foolish to repine over past mistakes which were made in good faith. Any fool can have hindsight; it is wise foresight that is difficult.

Do what seems best at the time, taking all circumstances, as far as you know them, into consideration, and then have no regrets.

Students of metaphysics of course always pray for guidance before making a critical decision. Claim that the Christ is guiding you; *and believe it;* and the ultimate outcome will be favorable even if things seem to go wrong for a time—provided you really do believe what you claim.

A SMILE IS AN INVESTMENT

Most people feel intuitively that the simplest things in life are the most important, or, if you prefer, that the most important things in life are found to be the simplest. This is a very profound discovery. What is more important to us than breathing, for instance?—yet we seldom give it a thought—fresh air doesn't cost a penny—and if deprived of air we die in a few minutes.

Another simple thing which is of great moment is *a smile*. A smile costs nothing in money, time, or effort, but it is literally true that it can be of supreme importance in one's life. A smile affects your whole body from the skin right in to the skeleton, including all blood vessels, nerves and muscles. It affects the functioning of every organ. It influences every gland. I repeat—and this is literally true—you cannot smile without affecting your whole body favorably. Even one smile often relaxes quite a number of muscles, and when the thing becomes a habit you can easily see how the effect will mount up. *Last year's smiles are paying you dividends today.*

The effect of a smile on other people is no less remarkable. It disarms suspicion, melts away fear and anger, and brings forth the best in the other person—which best he immediately proceeds to give to you.

A smile is to personal contacts what oil is to machinery, and no intelligent engineer ever neglects lubrication.

GREAT MENTAL LAWS:
1. The Law of Substitution

THERE are a few great laws that govern all thinking, just as there are a few fundamental laws in chemistry, in physics, and in mechanics, for example.

We know that thought control is the Key of Destiny, and in order to learn thought control we have to know and understand these laws, just as the chemist has to understand the laws of chemistry, and the electrician has to know the laws of electricity.

One of the great mental laws is the Law of *Substitution*. This means that the only way to get rid of a certain thought is to substitute another one for it. You cannot dismiss a thought directly. You can do so only by substituting another one for it. On the physical plane this is not the case. You can drop a book or a stone by simply opening your hand and letting it go; but with thought this will not work. If you want to dismiss a negative thought, the only way to do so is to think of something positive and constructive. It is as though in order, let us say, to drop a pencil, it were necessary to put a pen or a book or a stone into your hand, when the pencil would fall away.

If I say to you, "Do not think of the Statue of Liberty," of course, you immediately think of it. If you say, "I am not going to think of the Statue of Liberty," that is thinking of it. But now, having thought of it, if you become interested in something else, say, by turning on the radio, you forget all about the Statue of Liberty —and this is a case of substitution.

When negative thoughts come to you, do not fight

21

them, but think of something positive. Preferably think of God; but if that is difficult at the moment, think of any positive or constructive idea, and then the negative thought will fade out.

It sometimes happens that negative thoughts seem to besiege you in such force that you cannot overcome them. That is what is called a fit of depression, or a fit of worry, or perhaps even a fit of anger. In such a case the best thing is to go and find someone to talk to on any subject, or to go to a good movie or play, or read an interesting book, say a good novel or biography or travel book, or something of the kind. If you sit down to fight the negative tide you will probably succeed only in amplifying it.

Turn your attention to something quite different, refusing steadfastly to think of or rehearse the difficulty, and, later on, after you have completely gotten away from it, you can come back with confidence and handle it by spiritual treatment. "I say unto you that you resist not evil."*

*Matthew 5:39.

GREAT MENTAL LAWS:
2. The Law of Relaxation

ANOTHER of the great mental laws is the Law of *Relaxation*. In all mental working *effort defeats itself*. The more effort you make the less will your result be. This of course is just the opposite of what we find on the physical plane, but it will not surprise us because we know that in many cases the laws of mind are the reverse of the laws of matter.

On the physical plane, usually the more effort we make the greater the result. The harder you press a drill the faster will it go through a plank. The harder you hammer a nail the sooner does it go into the wall. The harder you work in digging the ground the sooner do you have a ditch. The exact opposite, however, is the case with thought.

Any attempt at mental pressure is foredoomed to failure because the moment tension begins, the mind stops working creatively, and just runs along on whatever the old habit pattern is. When you try to force things mentally, when you try to hurry mentally, you simply stop your creative power. To enable your mind to become creative again you must un-tense it by consciously relaxing.

In all mental working be relaxed, gentle, and unhurried for *effort defeats itself*.

"In quietness and in confidence shall be your strength."*

* Isaiah 30:15.

23

GREAT MENTAL LAWS:
3. The Law of Subconscious Activity

As soon as the subconscious mind *accepts* any idea, it immediately begins trying to put it into effect. It uses all its resources (and these are far greater than is commonly supposed) to that end. It uses every bit of knowledge that you have ever collected, and most of which you have totally forgotten, to bring about its purpose. It mobilizes the many mental powers that you possess and most of which you never consciously use. It draws on the unlimited energy of the race mind. It lines up all the laws of nature as they operate both inside and outside of you, to get its way.

Sometimes it succeeds in its purpose immediately. Sometimes it takes a little time; sometimes it takes a long time, depending on the difficulties to be overcome; but if the thing is not utterly impossible, the subconscious will bring it about—*once it accepts the idea.*

This law is true for both good and bad ideas. This law, when used negatively, brings sickness, trouble, and failure; and when used positively, brings healing, freedom, and success. The Bible teaching does not say that harmony is inevitable no matter what we do—that is Pollyanna—it teaches that harmony is inevitable when our thoughts are positive, constructive, and kindly.

From this it follows that the only thing we have to do is to get the subconscious to accept the idea that we want reproduced, and the laws of nature will do the rest; will bring forth the healthy body, the harmonious circumstances, the successful career. We give the orders—the subconscious does the work.

GREAT MENTAL LAWS:
4. The Law of Practice

PRACTICE makes perfect. This familiar proverb embodies one of the great laws of human nature and —being a law—it is never under any circumstances broken.

To become proficient in any field you must practise. There is simply no achievement without practice and the more practice, provided it is done intelligently, the greater will the proficiency be and the sooner will it be attained. This is true in the study of music, in the study of a foreign language, in learning to swim or skate or ski or fly. It is true in every conceivable branch of human endeavor. *Practice is the price of proficiency.*

In business life and in any kind of management or administration, *experience* is the form that practice takes, and here again it is practice that makes perfect. That is why, other things being equal, an older person is usually to be selected for responsible positions rather than a younger.

In metaphysics the effects of this law are particularly striking. Thought control is entirely a matter of intelligent practice. And true religion may well be summed up as the Practice of the Presence of God. But note that I said *intelligent practice.* Violent forcing is not intelligent practice, nor is monotonous plodding.

Practice is the secret of attainment. We might paraphrase Danton and say practice! . . . and more practice ! ! . . . and still more practice ! ! !

"Be ye doers of the word, and not hearers only."*

* James 1:22.

GREAT MENTAL LAWS:
5. The Two Factors

EVERY thought is made up of two factors, knowledge and feeling. A thought consists of a piece of knowledge with a charge of feeling, and it is the feeling alone that gives power to the thought. No matter how important or magnificent the knowledge content may be, if there is no feeling attached to it nothing will happen. On the other hand, no matter how unimportant or insignificant the knowledge content may be, if there is a large charge of feeling something will happen.

This universal law is symbolized in nature by the bird. A bird has two wings, neither more nor less, and they must both be functioning before he can fly.

It makes no difference whether the knowledge content is correct or not as long as you *believe* it to be correct. Remember that it is what we really believe that matters. A report about something may be quite untrue, but if you believe it, it has the same effect upon you as if it were true; and that effect again will depend upon the quantity of feeling attached to it.

When we understand this Law we see the importance of accepting only the Truth concerning life in every phase of our experience. Indeed, this is why Jesus said, "Know the Truth and the Truth will set you free." Now we realize why negative feelings (fear, criticism, etc.) are so destructive, and a sense of peace and good will is such a power for healing.

GREAT MENTAL LAWS:
6. What You Think Upon Grows

WHAT you think upon grows. This is an Eastern maxim, and it sums up neatly the greatest and most fundamental of all the Laws of Mind. What you think upon grows.

What you think upon grows. Whatever you allow to occupy your mind you magnify in your own life. Whether the subject of your thought be good or bad, the law works and the condition grows. Any subject that you keep out of your mind tends to diminish in your life, because what you do not use atrophies.

The more you think about your indigestion or your rheumatism, the worse it will become. The more you think of yourself as healthy and well, the better will your body be.

The more you think about lack, bad times, etc., the worse will your business be; and the more you think of prosperity, abundance, and success, the more of these things will you bring into your life.

The more you think about your grievances or the injustices that you have suffered, the more such trials will you continue to receive; and the more you think of the good fortune you have had, the more good fortune will come to you.

This is the basic, fundamental, all-inclusive Law of Mind, and actually all psychological and metaphysical teaching is little more than a commentary upon this.

*What you think upon grows.**

* See Philippians 4:8.

GREAT MENTAL LAWS:
7. The Law of Forgiveness

IT is an unbreakable mental law that you have to forgive others if you want to demonstrate over your
difficulties and to make any real spiritual progress.

The vital importance of forgiveness may not be obvious at first sight, but you may be sure that it is not
by mere chance that every great spiritual teacher from
Jesus Christ downward has insisted so strongly upon it.

You must forgive injuries, not just in words, or as a
matter of form; but sincerely, in your heart—and that
is the long and the short of it. You do this, not for the
other person's sake, but for your own sake. It will make
no difference to him (unless he happens to set a value
upon your forgiveness), but it will make a tremendous
difference to you. Resentment, condemnation, anger,
desire to see someone punished are things that rot your
soul, no matter how cleverly you may be disguising
them. Such things, because they have a much stronger
emotional content than anyone suspects, fasten your
troubles to you with rivets. They fetter you to many
other problems which actually have nothing whatever
to do with the original grievances themselves.

Forgiveness does not mean that you have to like the
delinquent or want to meet him; but that you must
wish him well. Of course you must not make a "door
mat" of yourself. Of course you must not allow yourself to be imposed upon, or ill treated. You must fight
your own battles and fight them with prayer, justice,

28

and good will. It does not matter whether you can forget the injury or not, although if you cease to rehearse it you probably will—but *you must forgive*.

Now reconsider The Lord's Prayer.

HAVE YOU A POCKET GOD?

THE Bible teaches us that "God is Spirit and they that worship Him must worship Him in spirit and in truth."* This means of course that God is all-perfect and that He is no respecter of persons. God does not favor one person in preference to another, nor does He ever help one person at the expense of another. God can always give us everything that we need without taking from anyone else. Indeed, the very desire to have anything that belongs rightfully to another is a serious sin, and is condemned in the commandment—"Thou shalt not covet." If you see anyone in possession of something that you would like to have, be glad that he has it; think "I am in touch with the source of that, and God can give me something as good or better."

Thoughtless people often try, as it were, to make use of God, without of course realizing the absurdity of such an idea. They try to make their religion do what they want. They try to use Spiritual Truth for their own convenience, instead of adjusting themselves to the Laws of Being. They pretend that God wants what they want, and that He wants it done in the way they happen to prefer. Very frequently, of course, they pretend that God wants other people to do things to please them. Such people are not worshiping the true God. *All they have is a pocket god*, trained to respond to their wishes; and such a heathen idol can hardly bring anything but suffering and unhappiness.

To worship the true God and to bring our lives into tune with Him is the only road to freedom, health, and harmony.

* John 4:24.

30

WHAT IS NATURE?

WHAT is nature? What we call nature is a small part of God's universe which we are able to see at the present time, and much of which we see awry. All the wonderful things that are going on in the woods, all the marvelous happenings that take place in the depths of the ocean, the whole sublime story of the heavens, are all parts of God's self-expression. Above all, our own bodies themselves are part of nature, perhaps the most wonderful part of all; and probably the part about which we ourselves know least. As time goes on mankind learns more and more about nature, for this knowledge is what we call science.

It is an irony that while man learns more of nature every day, while he knows the composition of distant stars, and understands the make-up of the tiny atoms, while he can irrigate a desert and harness Niagara, he is still unable to do the simplest things for himself—the things that really matter. He is unable in most cases to deal with fear, to overcome pain, to conquer some of the commonest diseases, to banish anger or depression, or in most cases to make effective use of his own mental powers.

All this is because man has been looking outside for dominion instead of looking inside, and seeking cause in what is really effect.

Dominion for yourself is to be found within your own mind. Establish peace there. Cultivate an understanding of God by seeking His presence daily, and you will find that outer things will take care of themselves.

"Seek ye first the kingdom of God, and His righteousness; and all these things shall be added unto you."*

* Matthew 6:33.

THE CAPTAIN IS ON THE BRIDGE

THE world is not going to the dogs. The human race is not doomed. Civilization is not going to crash. *The captain is on the bridge.* Humanity is going through a difficult time, but humanity has gone through difficulties many times before in its long history, and has always come through, strengthened and purified.

Do not worry yourself about the universe collapsing. It is not going to collapse, and anyway that question is none of your business. *The captain is on the bridge.* If the survival of humanity depended upon you or me, it would be a poor lookout for the Great Enterprise, would it not?

When you went to Europe on one of the great ocean liners, you never worried about your safe arrival—because you had perfect confidence in the captain. You knew that the Cunard or the French Line would not risk their ship in incompetent hands. When you woke in the night with the ship rocking you did not run up on the bridge and tell the captain to be very careful, or to mind what he was about, or to ask him if he was sure he knew the way. You stayed in your cabin and went to sleep again—because you knew that the captain was on the bridge.

The captain is on the bridge. God is still in business. All that you have to do is to realize the Presence of God where trouble seems to be, to do your nearest duty to the very best of your ability; and to keep an even mind until the storm is over.

"Great peace have they which love Thy law: and nothing shall offend them."*

* Psalm 119:165.

THE TIDE FLOWS IN AND OUT

WE DO not make our spiritual unfoldment in a steady straight line. Human nature does not work in that way. No one moves upward in a path of unbroken progress to the attainment of perfection. What happens is that—if we are working rightly—we move upward, but with a series of "downs" as well as "ups." We move forward steadily for a while, and then we have a little setback. Then we move forward again, and presently we have another little setback of some kind, and so forth.

These setbacks are not important as long as the general movement of our lives is upward. If each year finds us with a definite advance in consciousness, the temporary setbacks in between are unimportant; and if we worry too much about them they can be a real hindrance.

The tide flows in and out. Everyone knows how it does this. The foremost wave comes in and in, and it seems as though it would never stop until it reached high water mark—but it does stop, and actually goes back, and if one did not know better he would suppose that that was the end of the matter. But it is not. The tide goes back a little, but not to its old mark; and then it comes on again and this time it moves higher than ever, and so on. This mode of progression seems to be general throughout nature—an advance, a minor retreat, and then a greater advance; followed by another minor retreat and a still greater advance, continuously repeated.

Do not watch the individual waves but keep your attention on the tide, and all will be well.

"The joy of the Lord is your strength."*

* Nehemiah 8:10.

THEORETICAL CENTIPEDE

Do NOT dissect things too much. By the time you have dissected a living thing you have killed it, and you no longer have the thing that you began with. Take a rose out of the bowl, pull its petals apart, count them, weigh them, measure them, and then, while you will have certain interesting information, you no longer have a rose.

There is a place for analysis, but it is apt to be quite fatal in prayer and meditation. Do not dissect the love of God, but feel it. Do not dissect Divine Intelligence, but realize it. Pray more with your heart, and less with your brain. Do not wonder how God can possibly solve this problem, but just watch Him do it in His own way—and He will if you will give Him a chance.

Successful people in all walks of life do a great deal through the feeling nature, without arguing or dissecting. When the reporter interviews "the great man" and asks him for the secret of his success he can hardly ever tell him what it is. He does not know. He just does the right things because he feels them.

You know that God is Love. You know God can do anything. You know He helps you when you trust Him. So go ahead on that, and do not get theoretical about it.

Do you remember the old verse which says:

> A centipede was happy quite,
> Until a frog in fun
> Said, "Pray, which leg comes after which?"
> This raised her mind to such a pitch,
> She lay distracted in the ditch,
> Considering how to run.

Don't be a theoretical centipede.

USE WHAT YOU HAVE

MANY people say to me, "I want to get on faster. I want more understanding." And as a rule they go on to ask for a list of books to read or some "advanced course" which they can take.

This attitude is quite mistaken. It implies that spiritual advancement is a question of intellectual activity—of the mere accretion of knowledge.

That is true in the study of mathematics, or of physics or chemistry, for example, but it is not true in metaphysics.

Spiritual growth comes from putting into practice the knowledge we already possess. Instead of reading another book, read your favorite book once more and *apply it more carefully* than ever in your practical life.

To heal a cut finger or to solve a business problem by treatment alone, will teach you a thousand times more about spiritual things than the intellectual study of a whole library.

The one thing you have to *understand* and *realize* is that the world you live in is *a mental concept* and not an objective reality. Every true demonstration you get makes it easier to realize this truth, while intellectual study does nothing at all in that direction.

Metaphysics, like music, is both a science and an art. In metaphysics it is absolutely true that *you learn by doing.**

* See James 1:22.

HOW DO YOU FEEL?

REALLY there are only two feelings that a human being can have, namely, *love* and *fear*.

It is generally supposed that the kinds of feeling we may have are legion, but this is an illusion. All other feelings, so-called, will turn out upon analysis to be either *love* or *fear*.

What about anger? Well, anger is really but fear in disguise. In chemistry we occasionally find the same substance occurring under completely different appearances. For example, black lead is exactly the same substance chemically as a diamond, different as they look. They are said to be allotropic forms of carbon.

In the same way, anger, hatred, jealousy, criticism, egotism, are but allotropic forms of fear.

Joy, interest, the feeling of success and accomplishment, the appreciation of art, are allotropic forms of love.

The great difference between the two feelings is that *love is always creative, and fear is always destructive.* A sense of love rebuilds the body, lengthens the life, brings inspiration, expands business, opens the way in a thousand directions, overcomes any obstacle.

Fear destroys the body, kills inspiration, paralyzes business, throws a winter of death over everything.

It is for us to decide which of these two feelings shall hold sway in our lives.

"God is love; and he that dwelleth in love dwelleth in God, and God in him."*

* I John 4:16.

DIVINE LOVE NEVER FAILS

Divine Love Never Fails. Divine Loves Solves Every Problem. Statements like these appear again and again in metaphysical books, and, of course, they are perfectly true; but one does not always feel that either the writers or the readers clearly understand what they signify. Certain it is that many people firmly believe them, and yet have obviously been unable to prove them in demonstration. Why is this?

I think the explanation is that, consciously or unconsciously, people think of Divine Love as some sort of Power outside of themselves; probably up in the sky like the orthodox heaven; and they expect that presently, if they beg hard enough, this Power will come down and rescue them. As a rule they would not admit harboring such an idea, but I believe that some such idea is what they are actually entertaining.

There is, in fact, no such outside power, and therefore you cannot receive help in that way.

The only place where Divine Love can exist, as far as you are concerned, is in your own heart. Any love that is not *in your heart* does not exist for you, and therefore cannot of course affect you in any way.

The thing for you to do, then, is to fill your own heart with Divine Love, by thinking it, feeling it, and expressing it; and when this sense of Divine Love is vivid enough it will heal you and solve your problems, and it will enable you to heal others too. That is the Law of Being and none of us can change it. Now we see why criticism, grumbling, the nursing of grievances, the desire to overreach others, etc., are fatal to demonstration, because they prevent Divine Love from healing us.*

* See I Corinthians, chapter 13 and also the small card *Divine Love*.

THE PRESENT CRISIS

CHRISTMAS, 1941, finds us at one of the most critical moments in our history. In spite of every effort for peace on the part of our national leaders, war has been declared against us by three foreign powers. The American people enter upon this conflict with a perfectly clear conscience, knowing that it was not of their seeking; and they are united today as one man and one woman in their determination for a great, glorious victory. The great American victory that we know will come will be the best possible thing for the people in all countries in every part of the world. Meanwhile, each will do his duty with confidence, courage, and cheerfulness; calm and poised in the knowledge that the outcome is certain. Our slogan must be: Unwavering support of the government, and no hatred for anyone anywhere.

Christmas is a state of mind, independent of the outer picture that we see around us, and never was there a greater opportunity than now to serve humanity by witnessing to the All-ness of God in spite of appearances.

God Bless America.

THINK IT OVER

A SCIENTIST is one who asks, "How?"

A PHILOSOPHER is one who asks, "Why?"

A MYSTIC is one who sees life from the inside.

A MATERIALIST is one who sees life from the outside.

A POET is one who is a master of language.

A POLITICIAN is one who puts his party or his own career first.

A STATESMAN is one who puts the country first.

A PATRIOT is anyone who puts his country's interest above his own.

An ARTIST is one who makes beauty a religion.

A HERO is one who does the kind of thing that others are content to admire.

A GENTLEMAN is one who never takes an advantage.

A COWARD is one who sees the higher and chooses the lower.

A FOOL is one who thinks that the Great Law can be evaded (cheated).

A THIEF is one who tries to get something, on any plane, which he has not earned.

A GAMBLER is one who thinks he can gain something which does not belong to him by right of consciousness.

An ADULT is a person who has learned to control his emotions.

A YOUTHFUL person is one who is never bored.

An ELDERLY person is one who has lost the capacity for wonder.

A SAINT is one who loves God more than he loves anything else.

A Pharisee is one who uses God to glorify himself.

A true Optimist is one who knows that there is only One Cause.

A Pessimist is really one who believes in many causes.

A Quack is a doctor of any school who treats symptoms instead of causes.

A Crank is one who does not see things in the way that we do.

A sense of Humor is just an acute sense of proportion.

Criticism is only an indirect form of self-boosting.

Repentance is the gate of heaven.

Remorse is festering spiritual pride.

Religion is the individual's search for God.

If Brute Strength were the test, it is the lions that would have us in cages.

If Mere Size mattered, the dinosaurs would still own the country.

High Blood Pressure means high emotional pressure— too much anxiety.

Low Blood Pressure means low emotional pressure— loss of interest.

Creaking Joints come from a creaking mind.

The punishment of the Liar is that he cannot believe anyone else.

The curse of Ignorance is that the victim never suspects it.

The malice of Poverty is to have nothing to give.

The danger of Riches is a real tendency to selfishness.

The curse of the Sensualist is that the senses have murdered the heart.

The Perfect Man will be here when the perfect woman is here to claim him.

The man who overstresses his ANCESTORS is like a potato plant—the best part of him is underground.

People who are often late for Church MIGHT find themselves late for heaven too.

What we give to God's work comes back multiplied, and with a blessing. What we withhold from God's work can hardly bring us any good.

CHALLENGES

A PROBLEM is not a barrier. It is a challenge. The appearance of a problem of any kind in your life means that the time has come to take a step forward; and the taking of that step will, of course, be signalized by the solving of the problem.

The real step forward is always a *mental step*. The only progress we ever make is mental progress. All things be ready if our minds be so, and this means that all progress is a change of mind. The universe is always ready when we are.

Man discovered fire as an answer to the challenge of cold. If the whole world had been tropical he would probably not have discovered it.

Man discovered music as the answer to a desire for a higher emotional expression. He designed tools to overcome the many practical problems of daily living. The telephone and the automobile and the airplane are really but (partial) answers to the problems of space and time. The printing press is the answer to another problem.

In your personal life, a problem is a challenge. It is not a barrier saying, "You shall not pass." It is a problem—and to every problem there is a solution.

Find the solution through Scientific Prayer. Your problem will then be solved, and mentally you will have taken a definite step forward which will be with you throughout eternity.

The way to God is always open.

ONE THING AT A TIME

THE present moment is never intolerable. It is always what is coming in five minutes or five days that makes people despair.

The present job never tires people. It is work that is waiting for them that wears them out. If people would reflect that one can only do one thing at a time and therefore there is never more than one thing to do *at a time*, there would be less fatigue in the world. On Monday one can only do Monday's work, and for Tuesday's work—there is Tuesday.

Healthy fatigue comes from healthy physical and mental work, and usually one night's sleep is enough to repair it. Nervous strain is a different thing altogether, and comes from trying to do tomorrow's work today, or the task of 4 o'clock at 2 o'clock. Worst of all, it comes from working at midnight after a strenuous day.

The Law of Life is to live in the present, and this applies to both time and place. Keep your attention to the present moment, and in the place where your body is now. Do not have your body in New York and your mind in California, or vice versa. Do not have your body functioning at noon and your mind at 6 P.M. Do a fair day's work, and then stop. Overwork is not productive in the long run.

A friend of mine was visiting a great cathedral in Italy many years ago. Just inside the door was a magnificent mosaic extending the width of the building, but not yet completed. It represented the Last Judgment, and contained a great many figures, and the number of tiny pieces of different colored marble involved in it staggers the imagination.

A man was on his knees working away industriously, and my friend, who spoke Italian, whispered to him, "What a stupendous task you have! I could not even dream of undertaking so much work."

The man replied quietly, "Oh, that's nothing. I know about how much I can do comfortably in one day. So each morning I mark out a certain area on the ground, and I don't bother my head thinking outside of that space. Before I know where I am the job will be complete."

Sufficient unto the hour is the task thereof. *Now* is the day of salvation.

THE GREAT RUBBER LAW

THE great Law of Being is that we reap as we sow, that according to the thoughts we entertain and the things we believe, so will our experience be. This is a cosmic law. It is true on every plane and at all times. Being a law it is never broken. It is absolutely impersonal and inflexible, and to obey this law is the way into heaven or perfect harmony.

The whole metaphysical movement exists to teach this Law, and our progress is measured by the extent to which we understand and obey it.

All students of metaphysics know in their hearts that these things are true; but unfortunately they do not always act in accordance with that knowledge. They sometimes try to fool themselves by pretending that they can break the Law—and yet not pay the penalty. They pretend to themselves that if anyone else did it, it would be wrong, but in their case "it is different." They tell themselves that although they are thinking, speaking, or even acting wrongly it will not matter, because they will not count this time.

What could be more foolish, more childish than this? They have made a *Great Rubber Law* for themselves which can be bent or twisted in any direction, and they do not see that such a thing can only be an illusion in their own minds.

Fortunately we have to live under the Real Law whether we like it or not, and no amount of childish pretense or lame excuses will change it.

Have you made a Great Rubber Law for yourself?

If you have, scrap it; turn it in to the National Rubber Scrap Pile and start on a sound foundation.

Whatsoever a man soweth (in thought) that shall he also reap (in experience).

YOU CAN'T, BUT GOD CAN

THE spiritual forces that created and sustain the whole universe are available to help you at any time —provided you call upon them intelligently. Of course, there is only one First Cause, but it acts in a multitude of different ways and your response will always come in the way that is most appropriate to your need.

The way to call upon this Power is to become quiet both mentally and physically, and then to call upon IT quietly to do what IT knows to be necessary. Do not dictate ways and means.

Your prayers are not answered usually because you try to do the thing yourself instead of letting the Great Power do it. That is using will power and cannot succeed because your will power is only yourself.

Have you ever seen a heavy freight elevator in action or a huge hoist at the docks? You know what happens. The operator would not dream of trying to pull up that load with his muscles. He would tire himself out, possibly damage himself seriously, and make no impression on the task in hand.

What he does is quite gently to throw a small switch —and leave it in. Then the electric power without any effort or fuss raises the load to any height required, and as often as may be necessary.

When you work spiritually you are applying Infinite Power to your problem, and there can be but one outcome—victory.

"Be still and know that I am God."*

* Psalm 46:10.

NATURE IS FRIENDLY

"'She's a rum one is nature,' said Mr. Squeers thoughtfully, 'and I should like to know how we would ever get along without her.'"—*Dickens.*

NATURE, rightly understood, is that part of God's universe with which we have immediate dealings. Because God is Principle, nature works by unchanging Law, and she makes no exceptions, and has no favorites.

If we will learn the laws of nature and obey them intelligently we shall have health, freedom, and harmony; and as much power as we can possibly use.

As Huxley said, if we would command nature we must first obey her.

You will notice that Jesus in his marvelous works ("miracles") never tried to go against nature or to do "stunts," as we call them; but always fulfilled the Law of Being by bringing the patient more into harmony with the true laws of man's nature—for that is what healing is.

Train yourself to eat, drink, exercise, sleep, and work intelligently, that is, in accordance with the true laws of man's nature, and you will grow all the more rapidly in divine understanding. It is not spiritual to try to live in an unhygienic way. Nature is our friend; not our enemy. She is a kindly mother, always trying to protect and develop us—often against our resistance. She is not something that has to be vanquished.

Make friends with nature by working in harmony with her and she will make friends with you.

"God saw every thing that He had made, and, behold, it was very good."*

* Genesis 1:31.

50

DYNAMITE
(13 Sticks for Immediate Use—Handle with Care)

PLAN tomorrow's work today.
Review the events of the day, very briefly before retiring.

Keep your voice down. No screamers wanted.

Train yourself to write very legibly.

Keep your good humor even if you lose your shirt.

Defend those who are absent.

Hear the other side before you judge.

Don't cry over spilt milk.

Learn to do one thing as well as anyone on earth can do it.

Use your company manners on the family. If you must be rude, let strangers have it.

Keep all your goods and possessions neat and orderly. Get rid of things that you do not use.

Every day do something to help someone else.

Read the Bible every day.

These points may seem to be trite and obvious, but each one has hidden behind it, an invincible law of psychology and metaphysics. *Try them.*

CHRISTMAS*

CHRISTMAS has come around once more, and we find the nation passing through a time of great testing. Today the American people are called upon to prove their faith in God, and in those American principles which are written in our Constitution.

The response has been magnificent. Every section of the community has demonstrated its unshakeable resolve to make every effort toward the great Victory that we know will be ours.

People do not speak of making "sacrifices" today, for we feel that to forego, temporarily, some of our liberties and some of our comforts, is a privilege and a high honor.

Above all, we who have the Jesus Christ teaching rejoice in the knowledge that we can help those we love with our prayers; realizing that they who dwell in the secret place, abide in the shadow of the Almighty—and that they can throw the protection of their prayers around their loved ones.

Let us in the coming year keep the 91st Psalm very close to our hearts.

* 1942.

I f you have explored some of the back waters within a few miles of the ocean you will know how much difference *tidal water* makes.

Here you come upon a stagnant pool, partly covered with weeds and slime, an unpleasant place to be near, and an excellent breeding place for mosquitoes and other undesirable insects.

Not far away is another pool but this is filled with clean, salt-smelling sea water, and the growing things around it are pleasant and wholesome. Of course, the difference is that one is supplied by *tidal water* and the other is not. In one case the living ocean pours in twice a day charged with vitality, and then flows out again carrying away anything stale or lifeless. It is this circulation of life that makes the difference between the two cases.

In the tidal back water, when the tide is out, we sometimes see a boat stranded, lying on its side and unable to move, but we know that this condition is only temporary because the pool is open to *tidal water*, and the tide always comes back and re-floats the boat, when it can return to the ocean.

As long as you keep up your daily visit with God (call it prayer or meditation) your soul is open to *tidal water*, and nothing very much can go wrong. If there seems to be trouble it will not be difficult to deal with it, and even if you should seemingly be left high and dry for a period, it is only a question of time before the living ocean will float you off once more.

When you neglect your daily visit with God the tide

is cut off, and your soul becomes a stagnant pool in which fears and doubts and other noxious creatures of the mind can live and breed; and their progeny are trouble and suffering.

Keep your soul flooded with the *tidal water* of Eternal Life and "nothing shall by any means hurt you."*

* Luke 10:19.

GOD KNOWS NO "CONDITIONS"

GOD is not concerned with conditions. The unchangeable fact is that God has all power, and can bring harmony and healing out of any condition at any time and in any place. He is outside of time, and space, and the carnal mind.

It makes no difference to God how long a certain difficulty has lasted. It makes no difference how much seeming opposition there is to overcome—God is not concerned with conditions.

God does not have to prepare now, to bring something about next year; nor is He unable to do something now, because He omitted to do something else last year. God can do anything, anywhere, at any time, without reference to anything or anyone else.

Our carnal minds are always putting difficulties in the way of demonstration. We say "too late," or "too soon," or "too far," or "too near," or "too much," or "not enough," and so kill our demonstration; but all this is carnal mind thinking, and has nothing to do with God.

Determine today that you will demonstrate health, happiness, and true success, by realizing that God is working in and through you to bring these things about; and do not, for a single second, allow the carnal mind to tell you that it cannot be done. It can be done; and if you mean business, it will.

God is not concerned with conditions, and if you refuse to let them inhibit your thought, they cannot prevent your demonstration.

"With God all things are possible."*

* Matthew 19:26.

FREE WILL OR FATE

THE capriciousness of destiny was a favorite subject with the old-fashioned novelists. In their three volume world, people's lives were at the mercy of trifling accidents from day to day. A person's whole life was spoilt because one letter was stolen or went astray. The hero rose from obscurity to wealth and fame through meeting a casual stranger in a railroad car, or through saving someone from drowning at the seashore. One false step ruined an otherwise promising career. One turn of fortune's wheel solved all problems for someone else.

All this is nonsense. We are not at the mercy of accidents for there are no accidents, and trifles have only trifling effects.

In the long run you demonstrate your character; and you cannot ultimately miss the mark for which you are fitted, because of any outer accident. A particular incident may give you a temporary advantage or cause you passing grief or inconvenience, but it does not change your life's story. An energetic and enterprising man who attends to his business will make a success of his life whether he meets a helpful stranger in a railroad car or not—and whether a particular letter concerning him is lost or not. The miscarriage of a letter may deprive him of a particular position; meeting with a helpful and influential stranger may bring his success a little sooner; but if he has the qualities demanded for success he will succeed in any case. And if he lacks those qualities no help from the outside can make him successful.

No nation is destroyed by the loss of one battle. When a nation is weak in natural resources and divided within itself, it cannot stand; but it is this structural weakness that brings about its fall. If it were united, well organized, and armed, it could lose that battle and still win the war.

Your own character makes or breaks you. This is true of the individual, of a nation, of a party, of a church, or of any institution.

If you seem to yourself to be lacking in certain necessary qualities, if your character seems to lack strength, ask God to give you what you need—and He will.

You can build any quality into your mentality by meditating upon that quality every day.

KEY WORDS IN THE BIBLE:

1. Fear

THE Bible says that the fear of the Lord is the beginning of wisdom, (Psalm 111:10) and the beginning of knowledge (Proverbs 1:7). This has misled many people, because the truth is that fear is entirely evil and is indeed the only enemy we have. You can heal any condition if you can get rid of the fear attaching to it. Trouble or sickness is nothing but subconscious fear outpictured in our surroundings. It is true at all times that "we have nothing to fear but fear."

How then do we account for the texts quoted? The answer is that in the Bible the fear of God means *reverence* for God, not fear in the usual sense of the word.

Reverence for God is the beginning of wisdom. How do we show reverence for God? Not by fine professions or sanctimonious prayers, but by seeing God everywhere, refusing to recognize anything unlike Him, and by living the Christ life.

Confidence is worship. You worship whatever you trust. Are you trusting more in evil or in good? in fear or in God? What are you worshiping? That is the test.

"Acquaint now thyself with Him, and be at peace."*

* Job 22:21.

58

KEY WORDS IN THE BIBLE:
2. Wrath

THERE are many references in the Bible to the wrath of God. This puzzles many students of metaphysics because we know that God is Love and that the action of God always takes place to heal, to comfort, and to inspire. The explanation is that the word "wrath" in the Bible really means *great activity*—the activity that accompanies or precedes the healing of any negative condition. We know that while the spring cleaning of a house is in progress everything seems to be turned upside down for a few days. Also, when you heal a sick person by prayer he frequently gets worse before the healing comes. This kind of crisis is what is signified by "wrath."

In II Chronicles 34:25, for instance, we are told that the wrath of the Lord will be poured out upon the people because they have worshiped false gods. This means that when we believe in limitation and entertain negative thoughts, trouble must follow, but that if we treat, our treatment will undo the harm done and bring peace and harmony into our lives. This activity is the wrath of God.

In Psalm 76:10 it says "the wrath of men shall praise thee." This means again that the stirring up in us caused by our troubles leads us to turn to God and in that way overcome them.

The Bible always presents trouble and misfortune as ending in harmony and joy if we will turn to God.

"He sent His word, and healed them, and delivered them from their destructions."*

* Psalm 107:20.

KEY WORDS IN THE BIBLE:
3. I Am That I Am

I AM THAT I AM* is one of the principal Bible terms for God. It means unconditioned Being. It means the great Creative Power that is absolutely unlimited. It is an attempt—and a very successful one—to express, as far as language can, the infinity of God.

"I am" means you—the individual. It is an assertion or affirmation of existence and needs to be qualified in some way. We say, for example, "I am a man" or "I am a woman," "I am an American" or "I am a Spaniard," "I am a lawyer" or "I am a baker," "I am a Republican" or "I am a Democrat." In each case we state an important fact about ourselves, and to that extent we limit ourselves —not in a negative sense, but in a positive and constructive sense.

If I am an American, I am not a Spaniard; if I am a man, I am not a woman, etc.

Now God is absolutely unlimited, and the only phrase which can express this is I AM THAT I AM. I AM—what? I AM—pure unconditioned being, unlimited, and unspecified in any way. To affirm that God is any particular thing would imply limitation, or at least a circumscription, and God is unlimited.

It is man's business to be something in particular, and not to try to be everything, because he is an *individualization*. If you struck all the notes in the scale together you would only have confused noise. Music consists in the selection and special groupings of certain notes.

In God's universe each one of us has his place and it is our business to find that true place and express it—to

play our part correctly in the great orchestra. God, however, is the Great Conductor and the whole orchestra
too, unlimited and without beginning and without end.†

* Exodus 3:14.
† See booklet, *Life Is Consciousness.*

KEY WORDS IN THE BIBLE:
4. Salvation

THE word "salvation" appears more than 120 times in the Bible. It was in constant use among religious people of past generations, and while it is not so often heard today, the fact remains that it is one of the most important words in the Bible, and, as so often happens, it is among the least well understood.

The word "salvation," in the Bible, means perfect health, harmony, and freedom. When you have a strong healthy body so that just to be alive is a joy in itself; when you are living in conditions that are completely har-monious; when your time is filled with joyous and useful activities; when you are increasing daily in understanding of God, and are not conscious of any fear—you have salvation in the Bible sense.

These things are the will of God for man—for you personally; and the Bible was written to tell us how to attain to them.

We gain salvation by seeking God in thought, and letting Him work through us; by refusing to give power to outer conditions; by training ourselves to despise fear.

"The Lord is my light and my salvation."* "He only is my rock and my salvation."† "Thy chariots of salva-tion."‡ "He hath raised an horn of salvation for us."** "All flesh shall see the salvation of God."§ Such texts as these are typical of the Bible promises concerning salva-

* Psalm 27:1.
† Psalm 62:2.
‡ Habakkuk 3:8.
** Luke 1:69.
§ Luke 3:6.

tion. Habakkuk's prayer illustrates the mental anguish that often accompanies the activity (wrath) of God in our souls, when difficulties come to the surface to be cleared, and a period of stress comes before the demonstration.

Salvation comes to a few people gently and easily, but the majority have to work out their salvation with a certain amount of "fear and trembling" for the time being. The actual way in which it comes is not really important, for come it will—when we seek it with our whole heart.

It is an excellent treatment to look up the word "salvation" in a concordance, and then read a number of the verses containing it, interpreting them spiritually of course.

KEY WORDS IN THE BIBLE:
5. Wicked

THE word "wicked" occurs more than 300 times in the Bible and is one of the most important terms to be found therein. In the Bible the word "wicked" really means "bewitched" or "under a spell." The Law of Being is perfect harmony, and that truth never changes; but man uses his free will to think wrongly, and thus he builds up false conditions around him, and then believes them to be real. They look real, and so he forgets that it was he himself who made them, and thus he bewitches himself, or throws himself under a kind of spell; and of course as long as he remains bewitched in this way he has to suffer the consequences. Nevertheless, it is only illusion, or a spell, and it can be broken by turning to God.

The only way to break such a spell is to think of God, and that is why Jesus called it the strait and narrow way. "Oh foolish Galatians, who hath bewitched you?"* said Paul, when he heard that some of his students had begun to believe in evil in this way.

"The wicked flee when no man pursueth."† "The wicked shall be turned into hell."‡ "Let the wicked forsake his way, and the unrighteous man his thoughts: and let him return unto the Lord, and He will have mercy upon him.** These are all statements of what happens when we allow ourselves to be bewitched by our own thoughts into believing in any power other

* Galatians 3:1.
† Proverbs 28:1.
‡ Psalm 9:17.
** Isaiah 55:7.

64

than God. We flee when no man pursueth—we are afraid of things without reason. We can suffer the pains of hell because "fear hath torment"—but when we turn to God, the spell is broken and harmony is restored.

Let us awaken from the spell under which the whole race lives, and know instead that God is all Power, infinite Intelligence, and boundless Love.

KEY WORDS IN THE BIBLE:
6. Judgment

JUDGMENT, in the Bible, means deciding upon the truth or falsity of any thought. This process necessarily goes on in our minds all the time we are awake, and the extent to which we "judge righteous judgments" determines the character of our lives. To accept evil at its face value is to judge wrongly, and bring its natural punishment. To decline to believe in evil, and to affirm the good is righteous judgment and brings the reward of happiness and harmony.

Thus *The Judgment* is not a great trial to take place at the end of time; it is a process that goes on every day. When Jesus said, "Judge not that ye be not judged," he meant that to condemn our brother out of hand instead of seeing the Christ within him, is to put ourselves in danger, because we are making a reality of those appearances in him, and whatever we make real we must demonstrate in our own lives.

KEY WORDS IN THE BIBLE:
7. Heathens, Enemies, Strangers

THESE mean your own negative thoughts, which are the things that are causing your difficulties. They do not mean other human beings. Wrong thoughts are *heathens* because they do not know God. They are *strangers* to your real self, and, of course, they are the only *enemies* that you can have. All such enemies are to be destroyed, not by wrestling with them which only gives them power, but by righteous *judgment*—refusing to believe in them.

God is the only Presence and the only Power.

KEY WORDS IN THE BIBLE:
8. Christ

THE word "Christ" is not a proper name. It is a title. It is a Greek word meaning anointed or consecrated. It corresponds somewhat to the Hebrew term Messiah, and to the oriental word Buddha.

Jesus was the personal name given to our Lord by his parents. The word, as we have it, is Greek and is a translation of the Hebrew Joshua, which means, literally, "God is salvation"—that is to say, the realization of God is our salvation, or what I call the Golden Key.

Thus we speak of *the Christ*. The Christ may be defined as the spiritual Truth about any person, situation, or thing.

When you realize the spiritual Truth about any problem you are lifting up the Christ in consciousness, and the healing follows. Thus the Christ is always the healing Christ.

Jesus demonstrated the Christ in his own person and life to a greater extent than any other individual who has ever lived on this earth; and because the work that he did in his crucifixion and resurrection has made it possible for us to reach spiritual heights that would otherwise have been quite out of our reach, he is justly termed the Messiah or Savior of the world. For the same reason he is termed the Light of the world. The realization of the Christ heals, irrespective of any conditions or limitation that may seem to stand in the way.

"And I, if I be lifted up from the earth, will draw all men unto me."*

* John 12:32.

KEY WORDS IN THE BIBLE:
9. Repentance

To repent means really, to change one's mind concerning something. That is the true meaning of repentance. When a person realizes that a particular action, or a certain line of conduct, or perhaps the whole direction of his life, has been wrong, and honestly resolves to change his conduct, he has repented.

The Bible makes true repentance an essential condition for any spiritual progress, and for the forgiveness of sin.

Jesus said, "Except ye repent, ye shall all likewise perish."*

Repentance does not mean grieving for past mistakes, because this is dwelling in the past, and our duty is to dwell in the present and make this moment right. Worrying over past mistakes is remorse, and remorse is a sin, for it is a refusal to accept God's forgiveness. The Bible says that *now* is the day of salvation.

John the Baptist said "Repent ye: for the kingdom of heaven is at hand."† This means that you should change your thought and know that the Presence of God is where you are.

John practised baptism as a symbol of repentance. In his day it was already a very ancient custom among different peoples, because washing or bathing the body is a dramatic symbol of the cleansing of the soul by repentance. In the Old Testament the people washed their clothes before receiving the Ten Commandments from

* Luke 13:3.
† Matthew 3:2.

Moses, and in many other cases a ceremonial washing or cleansing preceded various spiritual exercises. This is the real significance of baptism and, of course, the ceremony itself is of no importance except as an expression in the outer of that change of mind, or repentance, or determination to do better, which is the inner and spiritual thing.

The law of life is to know the Truth and live it.

KEY WORDS IN THE BIBLE:
10. Vengeance

"VENGEANCE is mine; I will repay, saith the Lord."*
The spiritual meaning of the word *vengeance*, in
the Bible, is *vindication*. It stands for the vindication of
Truth against the challenge or accusation of fear and
misunderstanding.

We know that the real nature of Being is perfect, unchanging harmony. This is absolute Truth, and nothing
can change it.

Of course, it is possible for us to accept mistaken
ideas about the Truth, and as long as we do accept such
mistakes we have to live in their bondage. We also
entertain fear, and fear is nothing but a lack of trust in
God.

Then, at last, we decide to pray by turning to God
and realizing the Truth as well as we can.

As soon as we do this, the action of God begins to
take place, our fear begins to evaporate, and the false
condition is seen improving steadily.

Thus the Truth of Being and the goodness of God are
vindicated once more in our lives.

When we seem to have received an injury from
others, we must, instead of dwelling upon it with resentment, drive all thought of the matter out of our
minds, in realizing the goodness and harmony of God
in ourselves and the delinquent. This is *vindication* or
spiritual "vengeance" as the Bible teaches it; and it not
only heals the whole condition but brings great spiritual
progress to ourselves.

*Romans 12:19.

71

KEY WORDS IN THE BIBLE:
11. Life

JESUS said that he had come that we might have *life*, and that we might have it more abundantly.* The Bible often uses the word *life*, and always with the implication that it is the greatest of all blessings. "With long *life* will I satisfy him."† "Thou wilt show me the path of *life*."‡ "Keep thy heart with all diligence; for out of it are the issues of *life*."** Jesus says that those who follow him shall have the light of *life*. And the great goal of man is said all through the Bible, to be *eternal life*.

Now what is this *life* of which the Bible speaks? Well, we shall not attempt to define the word in this little essay. It will be sufficient to point out that you experience *life* only when you are happy, and feel yourself to be free and useful and joyous, and unconscious of either fear or doubt.

Everyone has known such periods in his life, though they are much rarer than they should be, and those are the times that you were alive—that you enjoyed *life*. At other times you did not have *life*, in the Scripture sense.

So when the Bible promises us long life, under certain conditions, it promises us a long period of joy and freedom. When it promises *eternal life*, it promises the enjoyment of these things forever.

A long physical life full of struggle, suffering and disappointment; living to an advanced age without joy or

* John 10:10.
† Psalm 91:16.
‡ Psalm 16:11.
** Proverbs 4:23.

hope—is not long life in the Bible sense. Such a history is really a form of death.

Life in the Bible sense is something supremely worth having, and we are promised it on the condition that we keep the Great Law—by seeking more knowledge of God, and putting Him first in our lives.

LET'S GET THIS CLEAR

You are, in your true nature, a divine being and you are one with God—now.

The Law of Being is perfect, unbreakable harmony.

You cannot know anything or experience anything except your own states of mind; and these you can change by intelligent and persistent effort.

You demonstrate whatever you really believe.

Any deed or any happening is but the shadow cast by a thought.

Divine Love is absolutely all powerful, and is not limited by conditions.

We do not pretend that we are not sick when we are; we say that inharmony is not substantial. It is a passing shadow cast by wrong thinking, which can be removed by the right thought.

The secret of happiness and harmony is Peace of Mind—and there is no other. You find Peace of Mind by getting right with God.

It is always a mistake to force anything. The right thing comes without violence.

This too will pass. Nothing in the material world lasts or is of transcendent importance.

There is positively no hurry.

As thy thoughts, so shall thy days be.

TODY IS NOT MORTGAGED

Your experience at any moment is the outpicturing of your mind at that time. What you believe and understand in the inner is what you experience in the outer.

People think that the outer things of today result from the outer things of yesterday. They think that what happens to them on Saturday is the result of something they did, say, on Monday, or at least—in the case of Truth students—they think it is the result of how they thought on Monday.

This is not the case. What happens to you on Saturday is the result of Saturday's thinking, pure and simple; and not the thinking of Monday or Tuesday, or of any time in your previous life. This means that if you think rightly on Saturday, Saturday must go well, irrespective of what may have gone before.

Saturday's thinking may result from previous events; indeed that is what will happen if you do nothing about it; but if you change Saturday's thinking, as you can, then Saturday's experience can be made harmonious and satisfactory.

Let us suppose that you get very bad news on Monday. This causes a feeling of depression and fear (on Monday). You anticipate tragic consequences in the near future. Perhaps the blow is to fall on Saturday. When Saturday comes you are thinking trouble, and the blow duly falls; but it is Saturday's negative thinking that produces the blow—not the event of Monday, or even Monday's fear. Of course, the world thinks that Saturday's misfortune was caused by something which

75

happened on Monday or previous to Monday; but the world is wrong. There is no cause-and-effect from the outer to the outer; it is always from the inner to the outer.

Each day is a new life. Each moment is really a new life. What we call memories are really present thoughts. What we call anticipations are really present thoughts. No one has ever lived in any moment except the present. To know this is the door to freedom.

"Behold, now is the accepted time; behold, now is the day of salvation."*

* II Corinthians 6:2.

76

YOU CAN IF YOU WANT TO

THERE is no true desire without faculty and no faculty without opportunity.

When you really desire to be or to do something, when you *really* desire it—it is a sign that God wants you to do that thing, and that He has signified his desire by giving you the necessary faculty. Indeed, that very desire is really the faculty itself making itself known to you by craving for expression.

People have all sorts of passing wishes, but a passing wish is not a real desire. In summer a boy wants to be a professional baseball player, but in winter he is going to be a ski champion; and for twenty-four hours after the big fire around the corner he is going to be a fireman. His sister goes to the Metropolitan and sees the bouquets being passed up to the prima donna and wants to be a singer; but a month later when a woman scientist gets the Nobel prize she thinks she will be a great chemist instead.

None of these are true desires. They are passing fancies. A true desire stays, and as time goes on it increases in force instead of diminishing. It is steady, and without excitement.

Build your true desire by thinking about it, studying the subject, seeking people and places in connection with it; and above all by claiming that God who gave you the wish will give you the accomplishment too.

Given the desire and the developed faculty, there is no need to look for opportunity. That door will open automatically.

Divine Wisdom now opens my way.

GOD CANNOT FIND OUT

GOD knows everything, and at all times. This means that God cannot "find out" something. God does not have to make experiments to see what will happen, as we do. God would not need to "test" anyone to see if he were honest or courageous or wise, because God already knows everything.

The Bible sometimes speaks of God as taking steps to learn something; or represents Him as having changed His mind or being disappointed. God is supposed to have tested Abraham's obedience in the matter of Isaac. God is supposed to have had His plans upset by the misconduct of Adam and Eve, by the general wickedness of humanity before the flood, and, in fact, He is frequently represented as being disappointed and even frustrated by the conduct of mankind. In orthodox theology, the devil was continually upsetting God's arrangements and bringing His plans to naught. Indeed, to listen to some preachers, one would have supposed that the devil was a good deal more powerful than God.

Of course, all this is nonsense. Of course, such things could not be really true of God. It was Abraham's *idea of God* that led him to prepare to kill Isaac, and it was his higher self, his indwelling Christ, that saved him from that tragedy. It was Pharaoh's idea of God that hardened his heart. It was the wickedness of mankind in the antediluvian world that brought on the flood as a natural consequence, just as the fears, hatreds, jealousies, and greed of mankind over many years have brought on the present war.

We make an idolatrous image of ourselves and call it God. Let us destroy this image today, and worship the true God who is infinite and unchanging Good.

TREATING BOTH WAYS

ARE you double minded? James says that a double minded man is unstable in all his ways,* and that such a person need expect nothing from the Great Law.

This is very obvious common sense. If you affirm one thing now, and the opposite in half an hour; if you think positively at 10 o'clock and negatively at 11 o'clock; if you meditate beautifully, and then go downstairs to talk trouble; it is entirely natural that you should fail to demonstrate.

If you stepped into a taxi at Grand Central and told the driver to take you to Central Park, and then, after a block, told him to drive you to the Battery, and then after a couple of blocks asked him to go to Central Park again, and then in five minutes changed your mind once more, you could hardly expect the driver to land you at any destination. Any New York taxi man would quickly turn you out of his cab, with no ambiguous expression of opinion—and yet this is what a good many students of metaphysics do in practice. They affirm both harmony and disharmony until the subconscious mind is completely muddled, and, of course, their lives are in confusion.

There is another way in which we can contradict and so neutralize our prayers and affirmations. This is by *saying* the right thing, but *doing* the wrong thing. No matter how fine our affirmations may be, if our *deeds* belie our *words* we are still treating both ways, and confusion must follow:

Every *word*, every *deed*, is a treatment. Where they

* James 1:5-9.

79

reinforce one another the effect is powerful and the result certain. Where they are not in accord they cancel out, leaving us where we started, or more likely worse off.

Put *all* your weight on the side of harmony, and results must come.

THE BIBLE HOLDS THE KEY

THE Bible is the most precious possession of the human race. It contains the key to life. It shows us how to live so that we may have health, freedom, and prosperity. It meets everyone on his own level and brings him to God. It has a solution for every problem. Incidentally, it is the greatest literary work ever compiled, and by far the most interesting of all books. Our common version (King James) contains the greatest and finest English ever written. Intelligent foreigners who wish to master the English language make a point of keeping the King James Bible constantly at hand and reading in it every day, and indeed this is the best way for anyone to acquire a good English style.

Nevertheless, the real value of the Bible lies in the spiritual interpretation. Wonderful as the "outer" Bible is, it is far less than one per cent of the "inner" Bible—the Bible that is hidden behind the symbols.

Hear a parable: A remote island was inhabited by highly intelligent savages. They had some primitive art, carved rough statues, and made excellent drawings of animals on the walls of caves, but they had no alphabet and had never dreamed of such a thing. A box was washed ashore containing a number of books, dry and in good condition. The natives were delighted with the windfall and they supposed the printed pages to be elaborate examples of pattern designs.

Their find included such treasures as a complete Shakespeare, *Huckleberry Finn*, and Wells's *Outline of History*; and they pored over these pages admiring the odd shapes and patterns made by the letterpress—totally unaware of the real meanings behind it all; unaware of the very existence of Falstaff, or Portia, or Hamlet; of Huck and Jim, and of the wealth of knowledge and instruction in Wells's fine book.

If you have been reading the Bible without the spiritual interpretation you are in just that position. You have not found the real message of the Bible, for that lies below the surface. The outer Bible is wonderful, but *the inner Bible is the supreme gift of God*.

"Ye do err, not knowing the scriptures."*

* Matthew 22:29.

We love him, because he first loved us.—*I John* 4:19.

Thou wilt keep him in perfect peace, whose mind is stayed on Thee: because he trusteth in Thee.—*Isaiah* 26:3.

In Thy presence is fulness of joy; at Thy right hand there are pleasures for evermore.—*Psalm* 16:11.

Behold, I make all things new.—*Revelation* 21:5.

Behold, now is the accepted time; behold, now is the day of salvation.—*II Corinthians* 6:2.

Seek ye first the kingdom of God, and His righteousness; and all these things shall be added unto you.—*Matthew* 6:33.

Behold, the kingdom of God is within you.—*Luke* 17:21.

Resist not evil, but overcome evil with good.—*Matthew* 5:39; *Romans* 12:21.

The letter killeth, but the Spirit giveth life.—*II Corinthians* 3:6.

Whosoever shall call upon the name of the Lord shall be saved.—*Romans* 10:13.

Look unto Me, and be ye saved, all the ends of the earth: for I am God, and there is none else.—*Isaiah* 45:22.

Ye shall seek Me, and find Me when ye shall search for Me with all your heart.—*Jeremiah* 29:13.

Whatsoever doth make manifest is light.—*Ephesians* 5:13.

But when he was yet a great way off, his father saw him, and had compassion.—*Luke* 15:20.

By their fruits ye shall know them.—*Matthew* 7:20.

I bare you on eagles' wings, and brought you unto Myself.—*Exodus* 19:4.

I Am hath sent me.—*Exodus* 3:14.

The house that is to be builded for the Lord must be exceeding magnifical.—*I Chronicles* 22:5.

He sent His Word, and healed them.—*Psalm* 107:20.

Mine age is departed, and is removed from me as a shepherd's tent.—*Isaiah* 38:12.

Thy youth is renewed like the eagle's.—*Psalm* 103:5.

Thou shalt have none other gods before me.—*Deuteronomy* 5:7.

These texts form a most powerful treatment.

BRAINS OR EXCELSIOR

You all know the Great Law. One way of stating it is to say: *Like produces like. Good produces good. Evil follows evil. What we sow in thought we reap in experience.*

If our all day thinking is positive, constructive, kindly, we produce health, success, and freedom. If our hour-to-hour thinking is negative, pessimistic, mean, we produce sickness, failure, and unhappiness. If our life is governed by Faith we become younger, more prosperous, and more joyous, as the years pass. If our life is governed by fear, the fleeting years bring age, decrepitude, and frustration.

People know that these things are true. They have not a shadow of doubt about them, and yet in spite of this transcendent knowledge they constantly use the Great Law for their own destruction. They would not dream of putting water in the gas tank of their car, or sand into their watch, or broken glass into their food; but they do something just as foolish every time they think, speak, or act negatively. Knowing the law, one cannot help wondering what such people have inside their heads—*brains or excelsior*.

Thank God we know the Great Law, because it gives us the key to life. All we have to do is to apply it, and while this will be a little difficult at first—like the acquiring of any new habit, or the learning of any new technique—yet practice will make perfect, and good results will pile up at an undreamed of speed.

In future, when you catch yourself thinking negatively, say to yourself severely, *"brains or excelsior?"* and immediately switch to what you know to be the Truth of Being.

THE KAFFIR DIDN'T KNOW

O NE day, about the middle of the last century, a traveller was journeying alone through what was then a remote part of South Africa. He spent the night in a native village, and the next morning, while smoking his pipe outside the hut, he noticed a group of little naked children playing what was evidently a native version of the time-honored game of marbles.

He watched the game idly for a while, and then something about the rough stones that the children were using caught his attention. They were quite small pebbles, dull, but—here his pulse began to steeplechase —he realized that they were really diamonds in the rough, and worth a small fortune in the market. He spoke to the children's father, with studied carelessness, and the Kaffir said, "Oh yes, the children like these little stones. They have some more in the hut," and he brought forth a small basket containing several more.

Repressing his excitement, the traveller took out a large plug of tobacco, worth perhaps twenty or thirty cents in our money, and said, "I would like to take them home for my children. I will give you this tobacco for them. Are you willing?" The Kaffir laughed and said, "I am robbing you but if you insist, all right," and the bargain was sealed, and not only enriched the stranger beyond his wildest dreams but led in time to the great discovery of the South African diamond fields.

This anecdote is of interest to us because the fate of the Kaffir is really the fate of most human beings. Man holds a fabulous treasure in his possession—the power of the Spoken Word—and yet, in most cases, he does not know it. He continues to live in fear, ill health, and limitation. By speaking the Word constructively he could obtain unlimited good. The treasure is his but he doesn't know it.

In the Bible, stones stand for spiritual truth. Let us pick up these neglected stones today and polish them; and let them glorify our lives.

HIGH OCTANE THINKING

IT IS the *quality* of your habitual thinking that matters. That is what makes or mars your life. It is not so much a particular thought, good or bad, but the general quality or tone of your thinking that determines your fate.

You may catch yourself thinking negatively from time to time during the period of self-training, but as long as the general tone of your thinking is positive and constructive, occasional temporary lapses will not matter much. On the other hand, occasional treatments can do very little if the general tone of your thinking is poor. *It is the general tone that matters.*

High octane thinking is like high octane gas. It means power and performance. In the new age, after the war, there are going to be opportunities for success and achievements in America such as have never come to any nation before. We shall find ourselves facing a new and better world, but the prizes will go to the *trained, constructive thinker*.

It is obvious to all that the days of special privilege are over, and that individual ability, and that alone, will count.

High octane thinking is the realization that God is working through you in everything you do—simple, but powerful beyond imagination.

If you really believe that God is working through you, the quality of your work will be so high and you will receive so much inspiration from Him, that every barrier in your path will fall away. Undreamed of good will come into your life and you will be a blessing to all around you.

High octane thinking means Power and Performance.

THE SECRET OF SUCCESSFUL SALESMANSHIP

TRUE salesmanship consists in helping the "prospect" to obtain the merchandise that he really needs. This point must be stressed. It means *helping* the prospect. It means *service*. It does not mean taking advantage of him in any way. It certainly does not mean forcing upon him things that he does not need and cannot afford. Nor does it mean pretending to give him one article when in fact he is getting another and inferior one. Such a policy is not salesmanship at all. It is, in plain English, robbery.

True salesmanship means finding out what your customer really needs, and supplying him with it; or if you cannot furnish it yourself, advising him to go elsewhere. Such a policy will not, as many would suppose, mean loss of business. On the contrary, this method— merely the application of the Golden Rule—will build up your business more rapidly than anything else could. People sense honesty and sincerity intuitively, and these things beget confidence. Working in this way you may lose one order through your honesty, but you will get half a dozen in its place—and you will have peace of mind. Every intelligent salesman should know that any particular sale, or even any particular customer, does not matter, that it is the annual turnover that counts.

Certain courses of salesmanship used to say, "Get his name on the dotted line before you let him go." You should do the exact contrary to this. If there is any doubt in your own mind, or in his, tell him to think it over and come back later. If he does sign on the dotted line, and afterward you have any reason to suppose that he is not entirely satisfied, you should offer to release him immediately, and tear up the contract.

This policy, the Golden Rule, was taught by Jesus, the wisest and most practical teacher who ever lived; and *it is the secret of success in business*. It is the real key to sales promotion.

Salesman! Treat your customer exactly as you would like him to treat you if the positions were reversed. Tell him exactly what you would like to be told about the merchandise, if you were the purchaser; and if you will do this the whole universe will co-operate to make your business career an outstanding success.

THE 13th HOUR

SOME wonderful demonstrations come at the 11th hour. Others come at the 12th hour. Some of the deepest and most far-reaching demonstrations come at the 13th hour—if you maintain the right mental attitude.

What, after all, is a treatment? It is simply the setting up of a new and correct mental attitude, as distinct from the old and incorrect mental attitude that caused the trouble. It is knowing the Truth of Being instead of accepting the error.

Many people are aware of this, and they work in the right way—for a while. If, however, the demonstration has not arrived a little before the 11th hour, they give up in despair, and naturally their prayer is not answered. But, this can only mean that they do not really believe the statements of Truth they are making. Their actual thought is, "These things are true if I get what I want very soon," and, of course, this is equivalent to saying they are not true.

If your statements of Truth are true, they are true whether you solve a particular problem or not; and they are true whether the victory comes at 11 or 12 or 1 o'clock.

State the Truth of Being concerning the problem. Believe it to be true, no matter what happens. Hold to it even after 12 o'clock has struck, and you will be surprised at the wonderful good that can come to you at the 13th hour.

WHY DID THAT HAPPEN?

WHATSOEVER a man soweth, that shall he also reap, says the Bible. This means that if we sow thoughts of health and harmony, we shall reap accordingly, and that if we sow thoughts of sickness, fear, and enmity, we shall reap those things. To sow a thought, in the Bible sense, means to believe it whole-heartedly; and it is our whole-hearted beliefs that we demonstrate.

You may say that you have a friend or a relative who is bed-ridden with disease, or has been the victim of a severe accident, and you want to know why such things should happen to him. You say that you know him to be a splendid Christian and a kind-hearted and open-handed man. Why doesn't God do something for him?

Such a question illustrates perfectly a misunderstanding of metaphysical Truth that affects many people. The Great Law says that we demonstrate what we believe. Now, your friend is doubtless an excellent person in many ways, and for that he will get his natural reward, but he believes in the reality of his sickness. He believes that his lungs or his heart, or some other part of his body is a material object with laws of its own, independent of his thinking, and subject to this malady.

That is his real belief, and so, naturally, he demonstrates it. When he ceases to believe these things; when he believes that his body is spiritual, and that sickness has no power beyond what he gives it in thought, he will find himself healed.

Trouble of any kind is nature's signal that we are thinking wrongly in that direction, and nothing but a change of thought can set us free.

We demonstrate what we believe.

WHAT? CUT MY OWN THROAT?

A MAN came to see me in London in great distress. He had attended some lectures I gave, and wanted advice.

He was the owner of a general grocery store in a village in the south of England, and hitherto there had been no competition. Now, one of the big chain stores was opening a branch almost opposite to him in the main street, and he was in a panic.

His father and grandfather had had the business before him, and he had spent his life in that one shop, living upstairs over it, and knew nothing else. He said, "How can I compete with them? I am ruined."

I said, "You have been studying The Truth for several years and you know the Great Law. You know where your supply comes from. Why be afraid?"

He said, "I must do something."

I said, "Stand in your shop each morning and bless it, by claiming that Divine Power works through it for great prosperity and peace for all concerned." He nodded his head in agreement.

I added, "Then step out on the sidewalk, look down the street to where they are fitting up the new store, and bless that in the same way."

"What? Cut my own throat?" he almost screamed. "Am I to help them against myself?"

I explained that what blesses one, blesses all; that treatment is creative, and makes more business—more prosperity—and that the only thing that could impoverish him was his own fear. I told him that he was really hating his competitor (through fear) and that his hatred could destroy him, and that blessing the "enemy"

93

was the way to get rid of hate. I finished by saying, "You cannot cut your throat with prayer; you can only improve everything."

It took some time to persuade him, but at last he got the idea, and carried it out; and when I met him several years later he told me that *his business had been better than ever* since the chain store appeared; and that they seemed to be getting on well too. He was prosperous and had peace.

This is what Jesus meant when he said, "Love your enemies."

THE LOCUST'S DINNER

And I will restore to you the years that the locust hath eaten.—
Joel 2:25.

Y ou can alter the past. There is no need to grieve
over mistakes that were made hours, or even many
years, ago. They can be changed.

This is a challenging statement. It may sound like
madness to the casual reader, but the student of metaphysics will take it in his stride because he knows that
what we call time is not a reality.

Perfect harmony is the Law of Being. Nothing can
ever change that. Any seeming evil, any mistake made
by you or by someone else is only a false belief (often
terribly real in appearance but still a false belief)—a
kind of dream. All there is of it is the belief in your
thought and that of certain other people.

If you destroy this belief in yourself by realizing
that only the action of God took place where the mistake seemed to be, you will get certain results.

You will forget all about the mistake. Everyone else
who knows about it will forget it too. All possible consequences of that mistake will disappear and everything
will be as though the thing had never happened. Who-
ever made the mistake will never wish to make such
a mistake again. The whole thing will have disappeared
from the race mind and will be *nonexistent*.

You will see that this is the "forgiveness of sins."
Here, of course, the word "sin" means any kind of mistake that one can make.

The years that the locust hath eaten is a false belief
of the present moment. The locust himself is only your

own mistaken thought and his dinner is a mistaken thought too. You are Divine Spirit and your life is hid with Christ in God.

This is the Good News.

MAKING YOUR DREAMS COME TRUE

MOST people indulge in some form of fantasy or day-dreaming from time to time. There is no harm in this as long as the amount of time devoted to it is not too great, but the important thing is to see that such day-dreams are *positive* and *constructive* in character. You are always thinking, when you are not asleep, and you know that it is in the selection of your thoughts that your destiny lies.

Do not let your day-dreams take the form of an escape from actuality. That is running away from your problems. It is a cowardly evasion, like drug taking. A day-dream is an evasion when it consists in fantasying something pleasant that nevertheless you believe could never happen because it would be too good to be true. Such a day-dream is a waste of time and soul energy, and it debilitates the whole mentality. Sentimentalizing about the irrecoverable past comes under the same heading.

Some people day-dream about all sorts of unpleasant things that might happen to them. They rehearse imaginary quarrels, imaginary injustices, accidents, and misfortunes of every kind; and because they do believe, only too strongly, that such things could and probably will happen to them, and because thought is creative, they actually bring them upon themselves in this way.

See to it that your day-dreams are concerned with such happenings as you would really like to find in your life. You know that anything good is possible; remember the creative power of thought; and *your day-dreams will come true*—to your great profit.

NOT DEAD BUT SLEEPETH

Most hotel rooms are furnished with a notice which says *do not disturb*. The guest has only to hang this outside the door of his room and he will be free from any kind of interruption. He can sleep in peace as long as he wishes.

Some people appear to have hung such a notice on their brains; and they deeply resent anything like a new idea, or even a new and better way of considering familiar things. Indeed, one might almost say that such people regard a new idea of any kind as a personal insult.

They are slumbering away their lives in a kind of semi-coma; repeating mechanically the time-worn phrases and threadbare ideas of the past, over and over without end. *Not dead, but sleepeth*, might very well be said of them, and, indeed, their consciousness is a mental cemetery.

If you have been sleeping like this, in a grave of defunct ideas and out-dated prejudices, pull yourself together, rub the mental sleep from your eyes, and live today in the living ideas of the present time.

Now is the day of salvation. Start right in today to handle at least one important part of your life in a new way. Break at least one rusty fetter today, and once this process begins you will be astonished to find how far you will go, and what wonderful things you will attain to.

"Awake thou that sleepest and arise from the dead, and Christ shall give thee light."*

* Ephesians 5:14.

98

THE UNICORN

Will the unicorn be willing to serve thee, or abide by thy crib?
Canst thou bind the unicorn with his band in the furrow? or will
he harrow the valleys after thee?—*Job* 39:9-10.

As LONG as we insist upon telling God His business,
nothing very much can come of our prayers.
When we dictate to God we are only using our own
intellect and will; and how can they make us any better
than we already are?

A man's problems arise because of some lack within
himself—and how can the same self that produced the
problems overcome them?

The ox, the mule, or even the donkey, will obediently
pull your plow and your cart, and take them exactly
where you want them to go; but you have to know
where that is, and how to get there.

The unicorn will not do chores. He will not pull a
cart or turn a mill. He will not follow a prescribed
route—he will not take orders.

The unicorn knows where he is going, and it is
always somewhere that you could not choose because
you never heard of it; and in your present consciousness you could not even dream that such a place could
exist.

Nevertheless, there are such places, and the unicorn
knows them, and is not interested in anything less. Some
day it may happen, probably when you least expect it,
that the unicorn will suddenly appear at your side, eyes
flashing, nostrils quivering, pawing the ground with
impatience. When that happens, do not try to put a
bridle on him, or to look for some task for him to do.

He will not do it, and there will not be time. No sooner, seemingly, has he appeared than off he will go again. So do not pause to think twice, do not turn to look behind you; but leap upon his back, for he is a flying steed, and he wings his way to the gates of the morning.

On that ride problems are not solved—*they disappear*.

NO GRAVE ROBBING

Don't be a grave robber. Let corpses alone. In due course Nature disposes of such remains, if they are left undisturbed.

Every time you dig up an old grievance or an old mistake, by rehearsing it in your mind, or, still worse, by telling someone else about it, you are simply ripping open a grave—and you know what you may expect to find.

Live the present. Pray about pressing problems. Prepare intelligently for the future—and let the past alone. This is what Jesus meant when he said, "Let the dead bury their dead." To think about the past is death. Every time you do so you strengthen, to just that extent, your belief in the time limitation, and you make yourself older and weaker.

God says, "Now is the day of salvation. Behold, I make all things new"—and God knows best.

Make a law for yourself today that you are not going to touch mentally any negative thing that has happened up to the present moment—and keep that law.

Life is too precious for grave robbing. The past is past—*liquidate it*. This is the great secret of handling grievances, blunders, and disappointments—*liquidate them*. You do this by simply writing them off in your mind, and refusing to consider them as having any present existence.

If a negative memory comes into your mind, cremate it with the right thought (the fire of Divine Love) and forget it.

Because the present is so thrillingly interesting and because the future is just as glorious as you like to make it, you are foolish to waste your soul-substance on what is really dead.

No grave robbing.

THE TWO SPIRATIONS

HAVE you heard the old story of the two spirations? They are essential for every worth while achievement of any kind. If either is missing the enterprise is doomed to failure, and if you have not been making your life as successful as you would like, you must go to work and find which of them has been overlooked.

I am sure it is hardly necessary to tell you that the two spirations in questions are—*inspiration* and *perspiration*. These potent twins are the godparents of all true activity.

First you need *inspiration*. "Except the Lord build the house, they labour in vain that build it; except the Lord keep the city, the watchman waketh but in vain."* You must have the godmother. Sheer hard work, blind plodding, or brutal hammering will not bring any success. It can kill you, but it will not bring success. You must have regular *inspiration*.

Secondly comes the godfather, *perspiration*. There is no success without persevering hard work in the direction of your goal.

Young people, especially, please note—there is no success without hard work. Recently I heard one of the greatest living musicians address a class of musical students. He said, "I know of no road to success except hard work. If there is such a road I do not know it." And he is at the very head of the musical profession.

When I heard this I added in my own thought, "Work hard—but do not make hard work of it."

* Psalm 127:1.

Contact God daily for inspiration; and then work hard but *pretend that it is play*.

This is the infallible recipe for success in any field.

THE SONG OF GOD

WHO are you? Have you ever asked yourself this question? Most probably you have not. Such a question would have seemed absurd because you took your identity so much for granted. Had anyone else put the question you would have said: "I am John Smith. I live at such an address. I am so many years old. I am the son of Henry Smith. I am in such a business." And you might add that you were a member of the right church and the right political party.

Well, these statements are correct enough, as far as they go, as a description of the picture you are projecting at the present time; *but*—and here is the rub—it is only a picture. It is all just a dramatization of your sincere beliefs about yourself. It is not the real you. It is but a passing unstable symbol of your current mental attitude; nothing more.

The real you is a spiritual being, perfect and eternal and incorruptible. The real you is the living expression of God Himself, expressing potentially every quality of God. "In His own image and likeness."

What is man? He is part of God's self expression. God sings a song, and that song is man. A song, as you know, expresses the whole nature of the singer. The singer's instrument is not just the vocal cords; it is his whole body and his whole mind. If the singer should be sick or tired or angry, these things would appear in the song. If his heart is filled with joy and beauty and Divine Love, these things, too, are expressed in the song. Man is the song of the Divine Singer, and celestial harmony is his nature.

Why does God sing a song? For sheer joy; not for any ulterior object, or for any sort of gain or advantage. God expresses Himself for the pure joy of living—because He is God.

This is the Real or Absolute Truth, but it is our task to demonstrate it, to bring it into practical reality; to change the limited picture that we *see* into the glorious Truth that we *know*. We do this only by letting God do it through us.

"I have said, Ye are gods; and all of you are children of the most High."*

*Psalm 82:6; John 10:34.

RUNNING AWAY FROM LIFE

IN THE spiritual teaching we are told not to dwell upon our troubles but, instead, to realize the Presence of God where the troubles seem to be; and we find that a little practice enables us to do this without great difficulty.

One or two of our critics have suggested that this policy is "running away from life."

Is it? Let us see.

Suppose you found yourself in an inner room of a house that was on fire; what would you do? Needless to say you would leave the burning building as rapidly as possible.

Now, would this be running away from life? Would it not rather be seeking life? Of course it would.

Sickness, sin, fear, and limitation—these things are not life—they are partial death; and they are to be overcome by turning toward life which is divine harmony.

Do we not learn from suffering? Yes, often; and some people will learn only in that way; but we still learn by *overcoming* and not by encouraging or accepting the negative thing. The man who accepts his trouble "with resignation" is not learning; he is steeping himself in more error.

To dwell upon negative things, no matter what the pretext, is to manufacture still more trouble. To turn away from evil and realize God instead is to improve and liberate yourself, to help the world, and to glorify God. The Golden Key is the key to freedom.

"Look unto me, and be ye saved, all the ends of the earth."*

* Isaiah 45:22.

NON-RESISTANCE

WHEN you fight a thing you antagonize it and it hits back. The harder you fight it, the harder it hits.

What you neglect, or, still better, ignore, begins to fade away or die by starvation.

When you give your attention to anything, you are building that thing into your consciousness, for good or evil.

When you are faced with some negative condition in your own life, the scientific way to handle it is to withdraw your attention from it by building the opposite into your subconscious, and when you have done this the undesirable thing falls away like an overripe fruit.

A wonderful story is told about William Penn. He had been accustomed from boyhood to carrying a sword at all times, because it was part of the dress of a gentleman at that period. One day it occurred to him that this was inconsistent with his Quakerism; but on the other hand he knew that he would feel extremely embarrassed in going without it.

He consulted George Fox, never doubting that his leader would say, "It is a bad thing. You must stop wearing it."

George Fox, however, did nothing of the kind. He was silent for a few moments, and then said, "Carry thy sword until thou canst no longer carry it."

A year or so later Penn felt that carrying it would be more embarrassing than going without it, and he discontinued the practice quite easily.

Do not tear away people's crutches (or your own). When they are no longer needed they will fall away. Dissolve the need.

Do not fight your rheumatism, or your debt, or your uncongenial job, or even your critical tongue (if you have one), but build health, prosperity, harmony, good humor, into your consciousness, and the unwanted things will disappear.

Re-read Philippians 4:8.

A BIBLE TREATMENT

THE Bible is full of powerful prayers and treatments. Some of the best known chapters are really treatments for healing and inspiration. The 23rd Psalm, the 91st, and the 27th, for example, are cases in point. You have probably known all of these psalms by heart for many years, but the way to use them effectively is to read them over carefully, trying to get something new out of each verse.

It is this getting something new that is the treatment, and it often brings a demonstration almost immediately.

Getting something new in this way is really *an expansion of consciousness*, and it is the expansion of consciousness that brings results.

"He sent his word, and healed them."*

* Psalm 107:20.

PRAYER DOES CHANGE THINGS

PRAYER does change things. Let us be perfectly clear about this. *Prayer does change things.* Many people say that prayer is a good thing because it gives us courage and fortitude for meeting our troubles. They say that prayer often gets a man out of difficulty simply by giving him self-confidence which he would otherwise have lacked.

Of course, this is not spiritual Truth. The fact is that Scientific Prayer—which is seeing the Presence of God where the trouble seems to be—does not merely give us courage to meet the trouble; it changes the trouble into harmony.

Prayer heals the body by changing the tissues, and it does this by first changing the mind which forms them.

Prayer changes environment by actually altering it, not merely by altering our attitude toward it.

Prayer brings man his salvation *by changing his nature* fundamentally; not by making the best of him as he is.

Prayer opens the way to new and better things. It does not patch up the old things.

The body, the environment, the universe itself, is plastic to our thought; and it always reflects our sincere belief.

"For as he thinketh in his heart, so is he."*

* Proverbs 23:7.

THE PACKAGE AND THE CEREAL

Your product is what matters. Everything else is secondary to that. If your work is excellent the battle is practically won. If the thing that you are offering to the world is worth while, the world is ready to take it, and to reward you liberally. If the thing that you offer to God is worth *His* while, He will take it, and reward you to infinity.

Packaged cereals are among the commonest objects in the stores today, and they illustrate very nicely the law we are considering. A successful brand always has two characteristics—the cereal itself is excellent; and it is put up in a suitable and attractive carton. Note these two points, and note that the first one is by far the more vital; although the second must by no means be neglected.

The cereal is good. It is what it claims to be. It is not a pretense.

Secondly, the carton is suitable and attractive. However good the cereal might be, if it were offered to the public only in large sacks or in wooden boxes (unsuitable presentation) it would have no success; and if the carton had a soiled or ugly appearance with blotty letterpress and ungrammatical copy, the result would be failure, no matter how good the cereal.

In practice, however, people rarely do put a very good cereal into a poor package. By far the commonest error is the opposite. Too many people seem to think they can palm off a poor cereal, if they will only make the package sufficiently attractive; and with this end in view, they devote all their energy to decorating the package, to the neglect of the cereal inside.

Such people think that smart salesmanship is more important than good merchandise. They think that bluffing and pretending can take the place of sound quality. They give themselves important airs or fancy titles or descriptions, and they think that this can take the place of substantial accomplishment.

Of course, this is a pathetic fallacy. Such people are devoting all their energy to the package and despising the cereal; and in no case has such a policy ever made a permanent success or even lasted very long.

Focus your attention on the cereal. Make the package attractive by all means, but remember that it is the cereal within the package that counts. Your success will stand or fall by the cereal.

"Whatsoever thy hand findeth to do, do it with thy might."*

* Ecclesiastes 9:10.

ONLY JUST STARTED

THE human race is just emerging from childhood. Its great days lie ahead. Today it corresponds to a child of twelve or thirteen years of age.

Scientists guess that man has been on the earth a million years but this is conservative. He has been here much longer than that, and civilizations have existed for tens of thousands of years—most of them now forgotten and their remains buried under oceans, and under deserts, and even under mountains. Yet, notwithstanding, the race is only in its childhood.

The great days lie ahead. All the greatest achievements of the human race are still unborn. The music of the future will surpass that of the great names of today, Beethoven, Mozart, and Bach, as they surpass the beating of primitive drums. Literature will be produced that will make Shakespeare and the other great lights of our civilization seem like children's story telling. The art of Greece, never since approached, will be overtaken and surpassed by new waves of spiritual inspiration.

Our greatest engineering feats of today, our bridges and dams, our high speed airplanes, our electronics, will be as toys compared to the engineering of the distant future.

Above all, man's understanding of spiritual things will grow by geometrical proportion; and the religious geniuses of past ages will be but pygmies compared with spiritual leaders of the future.

Turn your eyes to the future. The best is yet to be.

"Canst thou bind the sweet influences of Pleiades, or loose the bands of Orion?"*

* Job 38:1.

THE PERSIAN RUG

THOSE who are perplexed by the difficulties and seeming inconsistencies of life should remember that at the present time we get only a partial view of things; and that a partial view of anything never shows the thing as it really is. At any time we see only a particular section of the whole, and even that we see awry, through our lack of understanding.

If you were to show an Eskimo any number of pictures of sections of a horse, but never a picture of the whole horse, he would never know what the animal really looked like.

The old comparison of the Persian rug is an excellent one. It is said that if you saw only the under side of such a rug it would seem to be a meaningless jumble of lines and colors, without beauty or logic. This, however, would be only because you did not have the key. If you turned the rug over, you would see it from the right side, and you would recognize the pattern, and you would realize that these chaotic threads were really making up a beautiful and consistent whole.

So it is with life. Some day (when we have enough spiritual growth) we will come to see that the various threads that go to make up our lives, the seemingly disjointed happenings, the apparent accidents, are really part of an orderly and beautiful pattern; the warp and woof of something splendid that we are steadily weaving for God.

"Judge not according to the appearance, but judge righteous judgment."*

* John 7:24.

115

AN ADVANCED CLASS

MANY people would like to attend what they call an advanced class in metaphysics; and it will be worth while to analyze this idea briefly. What could an advanced course include that would not be in the ordinary lessons?

The usual metaphysical classes teach that God is the only power, and that evil is insubstantial; that we form our own destiny by our thoughts and our beliefs; that conditions do not matter when we pray; that time and space and matter are human illusions; that there is a solution to every problem; that man is the child of God, and God is perfect good; that Jesus Christ is the one who taught the full truth about God, and actually demonstrated it.

Once the student has obtained a correct intellectual comprehension of these facts, and digested them—at least partially—the only thing that remains for him is to develop his understanding by demonstrating them in practice. This, of course, is the task with which we are all faced.

So we see that *the real advanced course is the one we give ourselves by demonstrating* over the practical problems of everyday life—by attaining health, harmony, and freedom.

Every time we overcome a difficulty by knowing the Truth about it, God teaches us something new, and of priceless value which could not have been put into words or into a book.

We should all be working in the advanced class right

now, by the regular and constant practice of the Presence of God.

"Faith without works is dead."*

* James 2:20.

DON'T STRUGGLE

IN PRAYER or treatment (as in most other things) the less effort you make, the better. In fact, *effort defeats itself*. Pray gently, quietly, without strain.

When a person tries for the first time to swim, he nearly always begins by beating the water violently in his efforts to keep afloat. Of course, this is quite wrong. All that happens is that he tires himself out, and never swims a stroke.

Later, when he has been shown how, by an efficient instructor, he enters the water, and, with a very few gentle, almost effortless movements, he is at the far end of the pool. After that, it is only a question of time and regular practice for him to become an expert swimmer.

So it is with treatment. Turn to God quietly, with confidence and faith, and affirm that He is opening your path in whatever is the best way, or solving that particular problem. Let your prayer be an unhurried visit with God. Remind yourself that He cares for you, and that to Him nothing is impossible; and then give thanks— and expect results.

"For whosoever shall call upon the name of the Lord shall be saved."*

* Romans 10:13.

SEVEN POINTS ON PRAYER

WHEN you pray you plug in to the Power House. Daily prayer, when it is established as a habit, becomes an unbreakable life line.

The strongest prayer of all is an unselfish visit with God.

When prayer becomes a burden, or even a duty, it is time to quit.

If you are worried, or your mind seems water-logged, try browsing at random through the Bible, or your favorite spiritual book.

Be receptive to God. Do not be always telling Him. "Be still and know that I am God."

Pray gently. Don't try to rush the Lord. If you can get rid of the sense of urgency, your demonstrations will come much sooner.

KING HEROD

EVERY story in the Bible is a parable, while most, of course, are historical also. Consider the story of King Herod. He was afraid that a rival King would grow up in his kingdom and take away his throne. He knew also that it might be too late to fight him when he was grown and established. So he decided to kill off all possible rivals while they were yet babies.

This rather horrible story is a wonderful lesson for us, if reversed and taken in the right way, for it shows how we should deal with negative thoughts.

When a negative thought—a fear of something, a doubt, some resentment or condemnation—comes into your mind, *deal with it immediately*. Chop its head off there and then. Don't let it grow up to become strong and perhaps challenge your dominion, and even for a time defeat you. Destroy it in its infancy.

This is being King Herod for the glory of God, and is the course of highest wisdom.

When a negative thought comes, the first few seconds are golden. Do not give the evil even one minute to grow up in your thought, but—off with its head while it is still a baby, and keep your throne secure.

Never argue with false suggestions—off with their heads.

LET DOWN YOUR BUCKET

WE LIVE in the Presence of God. The Bible says, "In Him we live, and move, and have our being." This limitless power, which is Intelligence and Love—God—can be contacted at any time by turning to Him in thought, and allowing Him to fill our hearts. Whenever we do this He at once begins to influence our lives for peace and harmony and freedom.

Man wears away his life in the pursuit of outer things, when his salvation lies in discovering *the within*.

Too often we think of our salvation as being a greater or lesser distance ahead of where we are now, whereas in reality it is right here, or nowhere.

An old story is worth retelling. A party of shipwrecked sailors were drifting in an open boat on the Atlantic ocean. They had no water, and were suffering agonies from thirst. Another small boat came within hailing distance, and when the shipwrecked mariners cried out for water, the newcomers said, "Let down your bucket."

This sounded like cruel mockery. But when the advice was repeated several times, one of the sailors dipped the bucket overboard—and drew up clean, fresh, sparkling water!

For several days they had been sailing through fresh water and did not know it. They were out of sight of land, but off the estuary of the Amazon which carries fresh water many miles out to sea.

This old story is worth recalling, because it expresses beautifully the experience of many people who seek vainly for the good that lies, unsuspected and undiscovered, all around them.

Closer is He than breathing; nearer than hands and feet.—(Tennyson)

UNLOAD THAT CAMEL

Jesus said that it is easier for a camel to pass through the eye of a needle than for a rich man to enter the kingdom of heaven (Matthew 19:24, Mark 10:25, Luke 18:25).

Those who understand the spiritual idea know that Jesus did not bother with the question of how much worldly goods a man had or had not—what interested him was a man's mental attitude toward them and toward life in general.

If you are relying upon anything except a sense of the Presence of God, you are a fool in the Bible meaning of the word. If you are relying upon your own money, or your position, or your friends, or your human knowledge, or your own smartness, you are a fool, because these things will betray you sooner or later.

Knowledge, property, friends, position, are all well in their way, as long as you see to it that you possess them, and that they do not possess you; but if you want the Kingdom of God, you must be prepared to withdraw your *faith* from them and put it where it belongs.

The simile used by Jesus was a graphic one for his listeners. In those days every important city was surrounded by a wall for defense. There would be a large gate in the wall and this would be closed at sunset and placed under an armed guard during the night, in case of sudden attack. There was usually, however, a low wicket gate set in the big door so that approved travellers could go in and out at any time. This low gate was known as the needle's eye. When a laden camel arrived after sunset the only way it could get in was to be unloaded of all merchandise, whereupon it would squirm on its knees through the needle's eye and enter the city.

Unload your camel if you want to enter the Kingdom of Heaven. You do this of course, not by getting rid of conditions in themselves, but by getting rid of your sense of dependency on them.

Very often you will find yourself so glad to be without a lot of that merchandise that you will never put it back.

"Seek ye first the kingdom of God."*

* Matthew 6:33.

OUR ELDER BROTHER

JESUS CHRIST was infinitely beyond us in the degree of his unfoldment, but he was not different from us in *nature*. He was a human being, "tempted like us in all respects."* He is our elder brother who came on earth to show us the way and by his own demonstration to make it possible for us to follow. But he was human like ourselves.

This is what gives him his meaning and importance. If he were a god from outside the species, his life and work could have no significance for us. That a god did something unprecedented would not be surprising nor could it have any bearing on my life. When, however, I learn that a human being did these splendid things and went on to say that I could do them too if I would follow in his steps and pay the price, I am filled with interest and encouragement, and I want to put my feet on his path.

We do not say that Jesus was not God. We say that he was God but so are you and I. We are sparks of the Divine and therefore gods in embryo. And however unworthy or feeble we may feel ourselves to be today, we know that with understanding and practice, with faith and faithfulness, it is but a question of time—however long. Some religious teachers say that God is God, and Jesus only the best of men, thereby placing a gulf between them, but we deny the gulf and say that fundamentally and in our true nature we are all one with God.

"I said, Ye are all gods."†

* Hebrews 4:15.
† John 10:34.

SPIRITUAL HEALING

THE realization of the Presence of God will heal the body or solve a problem. Most people do not realize this, but it is true.

If you can *realize* the Presence of God where previously you were thinking of a damaged organ, for instance, the organ in question will begin to heal. It makes no difference whether you are working for yourself or for someone else, or how far away the other person may be; the law is the same. In practice most people find it easier to heal someone else in this way than themselves, but there is no real reason why this should be the case, and one should practise to overcome this handicap.

One should be clear that the *realization* of God does not merely prepare the ground for healing—it causes the healing directly.

The *realization* of God is, of course, a matter of degree. With a sufficient degree of realization the healing will be instantaneous. With a less degree it will follow a little later.

It is not often, however, that one gets a sufficient degree of realization to heal in one treatment. What happens is that the process is gone through a certain number of times, day after day, as may be required, the patient improving, until at last the healing takes place.

This is not the only method of working, but it is the highest. As we progress in Truth we should find that the number of realizations required becomes less and less.

Such a treatment may take only a few seconds, or it may take quite a long time, according to the temperament of the worker, and the particular conditions of the case; but it is not the time that counts, it is the degree of realization attained.

LIFE IS LIKE THAT

You form certain beliefs, for one reason or another—and then you have to live with them.

When you were growing up, well meaning people told you many negative things by way of warning, thereby implanting fears; and these fears are with you today, consciously or subconsciously.

Other problems you brought here with you when you were born.

You meet your fears dramatized. The things that we fear in our hearts have a way of coming to us in the guise of other people's acts; of business conditions; of a breakdown in some part of the body, and so forth.

Thank God it is not necessary as a rule to delve into the recesses of the subconscious and dredge for these things. That is the method employed by certain forms of modern psychology. In the spiritual teaching, as given in the Bible, we learn that by healing the symptoms spiritually (not, of course, covering up symptoms, but *healing* them) the fear or false suggestion which caused the symptoms disappears too, and the patient is free.

Pray daily for peace of mind, for wisdom, and for understanding of God. When some inharmony presents itself in your life, treat it away by spiritual realization.

The oftener you visit with God, if it is only for a few seconds at a time, the more happiness you will have in your life.

"Acquaint now thyself with Him, and be at peace."*

* Job 22:21.

THE GREAT BIBLE COVENANT

A COVENANT is a contract. When two people enter into a covenant, it means that one party undertakes to do certain things provided the other party does certain other things. Thus it is a mutual agreement.

The Bible has a good deal to say about a certain covenant—indeed the word itself occurs well over 200 times in the Bible—and it is of the greatest importance that we understand what this covenant is.

The Bible covenant is a contract that exists between God and each member of the human race. God says that you can have health, freedom, happiness, true prosperity, perfect peace, and constant spiritual growth—*provided* that you train yourself to think only harmonious thoughts and to believe only in the law of good.

If you will think only kindly, optimistic, and constructive thoughts, if you will speak only positive and helpful words *at all times*, if you will do only good and constructive deeds, you will be fulfilling your side of the great covenant—and in no circumstances could God fail to fulfil His.

Of course this reference to a covenant or legal document is a figure of speech under which the Bible explains the great psychological and metaphysical Law of Life.

"Keep therefore the words of this covenant, and do them, that ye may prosper in all that ye do."*

* Deuteronomy 29:9.

128

FEEDING AND STARVING

Iᴛ is said that living creatures always follow their food, and doubtless this is true. Animal life is rare, or altogether absent, in regions where food is usually unobtainable. On the other hand, all kinds of life swarm where nourishment is plentiful. Slovenly housekeepers attract rats, mice, and other low forms of life by letting scraps of food accumulate in closets and by a general lack of cleanliness.

Events and experiences are living things too, and they also seek and follow after their food. *The food of events is thought.* Your habitual thoughts nourish your conditions and cause them to increase and multiply.

Fear thoughts, gloomy and critical thoughts, selfish thoughts, are the food of unhappiness, sickness, and failure. When you supply this food in abundance these things come into your life—because they seek their food.

Thoughts of God, thoughts of kindness, of optimism, and good will, are the food of health, joy, and success; and if you furnish a bountiful supply of this food you will attract these things instead.

When you want to get some condition out of your life, *starve it out* by refusing to furnish any of the food upon which it thrives, and you will be surprised how rapidly it will leave you. It will go away in a hurry somewhere else, where its food is obtainable.

"I am the bread of life."*

* John 6:35.

129

"GIVE ME AN AFFIRMATION"

PEOPLE sometimes ask me to give them an affirmation, apparently under the impression that repeating a magic phrase is going to solve their problem—but nothing could be farther from the truth.

Your problem is with you owing to a mistaken belief or process of thought. The only way to get rid of your problem is to change your belief, or reverse the false process of thought.

Fear is always present where there is inharmony, and an affirmation will not in itself destroy fear. You must refuse to be intimidated by the seeming danger, whatever it is, and put your reliance on the Love of God. Then fear will begin to go.

When you need guidance for an important decision, the way to get it is to think and believe that God is guiding you, and this belief will bring your guidance.

An affirmation is often helpful as a *memorandum* of what you are to believe, but it is the change in your process of thinking from error to Truth that brings the demonstration—not just the repetition of a phrase.

"When ye pray, use not vain repetitions, as the heathen do."*

* Matthew 6:7.

130

REALIZATION IS THE KEY

THERE is a big difference between what you really believe, and what you think you ought to believe, or what you want to believe.

You demonstrate what you really believe. The other ideas do not demonstrate. If, some day, you do come to believe them, they will then demonstrate, or come into effect in your life—but not before.

It is not much use saying that you know that a thing will not hurt you if you only know it intellectually. If you *realize* even slightly that it cannot hurt you, the case is different, but just saying in a perfunctory way that a thing cannot hurt you is not enough.

It is not enough to say that you will be all right, unless you believe it. It is not enough to say that God will take care of you, unless you realize and believe what you are saying, to at least a small degree.

The sole object of spiritual treatment is to increase your *realization* of the truth which you already accept; namely that God can and will protect you from all harm, and that fear and error have no power when you yourself do not give it to them.

"Nothing shall by any means hurt you."*

* Luke 10:19.

131

HE USED TO DEMONSTRATE

PEOPLE often say that when they first came to the knowledge of metaphysical truth it seemed that miracles happened almost every day. Negative conditions of long standing disappeared after a short treatment. Then, they say, that a sort of slump seemed to set in, since which they have never been able to do so well.

Now why should this be the case? The explanation is that what demonstrates is an *expansion of consciousness*.

When we bring about an expansion of consciousness our conditions must improve. When people first learn of the omnipresence of God, and the unreality of evil, they experience such an expansion—and they demonstrate remarkably.

Then the tendency is, so to speak, to rest upon the first knowledge acquired, and to make their early realization serve over and over again.

This will not do. It is only today's realization that will demonstrate, never yesterday's or last year's.

If you want to demonstrate today you must, in some way, gain an expansion or upliftment of consciousness just as you did in the beginning. You must learn a little more about God; and that is the real object of prayer and treatment.

"God is not the God of the dead, but of the living."*

* Matthew 22:32.

THE KEY TO THE BIBLE

THE Bible deals with states of mind—and the results which those states of mind produce.*

Each character in the Bible represents a particular state of mind, and the leading events in the Bible describe the consequences following upon certain states of mind.

His faith and understanding get Moses out of Egypt,† and get Peter out of prison,‡ and these qualities will liberate anyone else in the same way, whether it be a prison of sin, of fear, of doubt, or some other human limitation.

Any text in the Bible can be taken in the present, the past, or the future tense—because God is outside of time.

The heroes of the Bible are represented as having many faults in the beginning, which they gradually overcome by the practice of prayer. This is very encouraging for us.

The Bible teaches that outer conditions and events are not important in themselves, but only in so far as they necessarily express the character (consciousness) of the subject.

The Bible is infinitely optimistic but never Pollyanna. It says, Thou wilt keep him in perfect peace, whose mind is stayed on thee."** But it also teaches that negative thoughts and beliefs, especially the sin of limiting God,§ can bring all kinds of trouble and suffering in their train.

* See booklet, *Adam and Eve*, page 12.
† Exodus 14:21.
‡ Acts 12:7.
** Isaiah 26:3.
§ Psalm 78:41.

133

The Bible teaches that *today's prayer can put everything right*—if only you will not look back to yesterday—remember Lot's wife.

Do not postpone reading the Bible until you "have plenty of time and can do it thoroughly," but start today and read a little—even a few verses—daily.

GOD IS NOT BECOMING

Gᴏᴅ is infinite perfection and He is not concerned with our limited ideas about time and space and matter. He is the High and Lofty One that inhabiteth eternity, whose name is Holy (perfect).*

God is not progressing or improving. What improves is our understanding of Him, and as this happens all our conditions necessarily improve too.

There never was a time in your history when God was not all that He is today, and there never can come a time when God will be any more than He is today.

Anything that you can need is part of God's expression for you *at this moment*. Indeed, what we call a need or a wish is really but our rather clouded sensing of the presence of the thing itself.

There is no lack in Divine Mind—all lack is but your failure to realize the Presence of God at that point.

There are no delays for the Holy One that inhabiteth eternity. You are His expression, and what you call delay is still but your failure to realize present good.

God is continually expressing Himself in new ways—but this is not improvement; it is unfoldment. Your life is simply part of this unfoldment, and that is the only reason for your existing at all.

You are the living expression of God now—and to understand this is salvation.

* Isaiah 57:15.

IN TIME OF DANGER

IN TIME of danger, the best prayer or treatment is quietly to be aware of the protecting power of God's love.

In spite of our prayers, conditions sometimes seem to grow worse, but this is the very time to hold strongly to the Truth. If we cannot hold to the Truth in face of negative appearances, what is our faith in God worth? By holding steadily to the Truth in spite of difficulties, we shall presently find ourselves in safety.

Many people have faith enough to call upon God and to trust him for a while, but if the response is not immediate, their faith breaks down, and they lose their demonstration. Peter trying to walk upon the water* is a splendid example of this.

Any prayer, any text that helps you to realize in some degree the love and presence of God, is a protection against danger. In particular, the 91st Psalm should be studied constantly by those who are exposed to danger themselves, and by those whose loved ones may be so. The fact that you have probably known this psalm by heart since you were a child makes no difference. Try to get something new out of each verse each time that you use it.

"Whosoever shall call upon the name of the Lord shall be saved."†

* Matthew 14:29-31.
† Romans 10:13.

How often should one treat about a certain problem? Is one treatment enough? How long should a treatment last?

These questions constantly present themselves, and they are very important. In fact, our general success in prayer will depend largely on the answers which we give to them in our own minds.

You cannot make universal rules for treatment. The problem, the surrounding conditions, and the individual concerned have to be taken into account. The same person has to work differently at different times. The following indications, however, will be found of general use.

One treatment is hardly ever enough, particularly if it concerns something which you consider important.

The right length for a treatment depends on the temperament of the individual, and on the state of mind that he happens to be in at the time. The correct practice is to treat until you feel satisfied or until you feel that you can do no more for the time being. When you stop, do not think "this will do for the present; I will come back to it later"—this stultifies your treatment—but expect *that* treatment to demonstrate.

You may treat again as soon as you have gotten away from the last treatment—but not before. You have gotten away from the last treatment when you have forgotten about the whole subject for some time, say, at least half an hour. That is to say, if you treat about something at ten o'clock, and then, because you are busy about other things, you forget the whole subject (it goes completely out of your conscious mind) for at least half an hour (or it might be a couple of hours), then, when you think of it again, you may treat once again, and so on.

Many people find it better to treat about a problem once a day, or possibly morning and evening. The important thing is to avoid nagging at the problem from time to time all day long. That may postpone demonstration indefinitely. Lightness of touch is the principal secret of success.

Always remind yourself that it is God who is making the prayer *through* you.

"He sends His word, and heals them."*

* Psalm 107:20.

CROSSING BROOKLYN BRIDGE

W HEN you are praying or treating for your *true place*, it is well to remember that the full demonstration may not come in one move, but more likely after a series of stages. These intermediate steps should be welcomed one by one for what they are—stepping stones to the complete demonstration.

Whether it is right occupation, or an ideal home, or perfect personal arrangements of some other kind, the chances are that you will progress by steps.

Now, if you despise these intermediate steps, and think "this is a little better, but it is not really what I want," you will keep the demonstration back. Neither should you accept a small improvement as being all that you can hope to get. The scientific attitude is to see the stepping stone *as* a stepping stone; to bless it, and give thanks for it, and to continue praying for the next step.

If you were in Brooklyn and you wanted to reach Manhattan, you would cross the Brooklyn Bridge. You would be thankful to find yourself on the bridge because that would mean that you were on your way. You would not say, "I did not want to be on this bridge. I wanted to be in Manhattan." Neither would you say, "This will do. I suppose I will have to stay here forever." You would regard the time spent on the bridge as well employed because it was taking you to your destination.

Every small improvement is a part of the bridge between today's location and your heart's desire.

"In quietness and in confidence shall be your strength."*

* Isaiah 30:15.

APPRAISAL

PROFESSIONAL appraisers exist in various fields. An expert will come in, take a good look at certain merchandise, and put an estimated value upon it. It is interesting to observe how often this verdict is found, by the market test, to be about correct.

We seldom realize it, but we all do just that whenever a new problem faces us. We take a quick look at it, and we appraise its importance—but we nearly always *overrate* it enormously.

A three-ounce difficulty we appraise at three tons (or sometimes even three hundred tons) through *fear*.

Now, the size of any difficulty, or any problem, for *you*, is the size at which *you* appraise it.

What you *really* consider to be a big problem, is a big problem for you. What you *really* consider a small problem, is a small problem for you. Of course, the higher the value at which you appraise the problem, the lower the value at which you appraise the power of God.

We are told that, to the wise, a word is sufficient.

According to your faith shall it be done unto you.

THE PRAYER THAT BRINGS RESULTS

THE prayer that works is simple, direct, and spontaneous. Jesus said that in prayer we should approach God in the way that small children approach their parents.

Short prayers are nearly always better than long prayers.

Pray, if only for a moment, many times during the day.

Remember that prayer means thinking of God. If you are thinking about yourself, or your troubles, or about somebody else, you are not at that moment praying.

If you are primarily interested in your spiritual development, and regard your outer conditions as only incidental, such conditions will improve much faster than if you are primarily interested in improving your conditions, and regard your spiritual growth as only incidental.

Peace of mind, a healthy body, and harmonious surroundings are important for the reason that such things are the proof of spiritual understanding.

Remember that the great spiritual Power House is the Bible.

WORDS, WORDS, WORDS

WHEN you apply a certain word to God, it must bear the same essential meaning as it does when you apply it to man—otherwise it has no meaning at all.

When you say that God is *Love* or *Intelligence*, or that He is *just*, these words must mean substantially what they mean when applied to human beings—or else they are new and special words which therefore carry no significance whatever.

The love of God must be essentially the same thing that we know as the love of the mother for her child, or the love of the artist for his creation, for example. It must be the same quality as these—purified and increased to infinity, of course—but still the same thing in quality; or the term has simply no meaning.

When we say that God is just, we must mean the same kind of thing that we mean when we say that a certain magistrate, or anyone else in authority, acts with justice—or the word has no meaning at all. The justice of God will include an infinite perspective and be quite flawless, but it will be essentially the same thing in its nature.

Many people say that God is *Love*, and at the same time maintain that He visits finite sin with eternal punishment. They claim that God is *just*, and yet maintain that people living today are suffering disabilities for a sin supposed to have been committed by Adam thousands of years before they were born. There is still a small number of people who believe that every human being was predestined to heaven or hell before he was created at all, and that his conduct, good or bad while on this earth, would make no difference to his fate. And the same people say that God is *just*. Obviously in such cases these terms can have no meaning.

If the attributes of God are supposed to signify something different from that conveyed by the ordinary meaning of the words, we cannot know what such meaning is. You might as well say, "God is x+y, but I do not know what these symbols stand for."

The truth is that God *is* Love and Intelligence; and that He works with perfect wisdom and perfect justice to all, at all times, in the ordinary and correct meaning of these words.

"God is light, and in Him is no darkness at all."*

* 1 John 1:5.

SEVEN POWERFUL PRAYERS

Twenty-third Psalm. Use this chapter when you need something of importance. You know it by heart but *read* it and get something new from it. This new inspiration brings the result.

Ninety-first Psalm. Read when you feel a sense of danger or apprehension. The note about the 23rd Psalm applies to this one also.

Daniel, Chapter 6. Read this chapter when your difficulties are actually with you, and seem to be almost immovable.

Hebrews, Chapter 2. This is the chapter for handling doubts and discouragement.

James, Chapter 1. Packed with psychology and metaphysics. A course of instruction in itself. James is profound, very practical, and rather personal.

Exodus, Chapter 15. A song of triumph—of thanksgiving for prayer answered. Thanksgiving (before the demonstration arrives—or is even in sight) is a most powerful form of prayer.

1 Corinthians, Chapter 13. The fulfilling of the law. The shortest cut to Health, Harmony, and Success. The Golden Gate.

YOUR MENTAL ASSENT

WHEN you give your mental assent to any idea, good or bad, you associate yourself with that idea and you incorporate it into your consciousness—to the extent that you realize it.

When you listen to an audible treatment, or read a passage of Scripture you will, if you assent to it mentally, incorporate it into your life to that extent, and you will benefit accordingly.

This law, of course, works the other way too. If when you hear or read of some piece of injustice or cruelty, you approve it mentally by thinking that "it serves him right," etc., you are associating yourself with that deed, and making it part of your own life, even though you do not speak a word.

It is the mental assent that counts.

Do not associate yourself in thought with any negative or evil thing under any pretense, and thus you will keep your own consciousness clear and harmonious.

Join yourself, by your habitual mental tuning, to infinite goodness and beauty that is always surrounding you. *Give your assent only to Truth.*

SEVEN BASIC POINTS

THERE is only one CAUSE, the great Creative Spirit— God.

God is and has INFINITE INTELLIGENCE. God knows everything. God has all power, and can do anything at any time irrespective of conditions.

The nature or character of God is PERFECT GOODNESS and PERFECT LOVE. God acts only to heal, to liberate, to inspire.

You are a center for the expression of God where you are. You are an individualization of God but you have to discover and gradually realize this fact.

You surround yourself with the image and likeness of yourself, as Emerson said. Your real beliefs (mostly subconscious) are expressed in your body and surroundings.

If you are doing your best to live the spiritual life, it is probable that most of your difficulties today are not caused by present wrong thinking, but came out of the distant past. They are coming out to be cleared up that you may be free of them forever.

Your troubles are not necessarily due to sin in the present or the past, but are more often caused by lack of knowledge or by well intentioned mistakes. The result of sin is much harder to wipe out, but it can be done just as completely, if the sin is abandoned.

RAISE THE SHADES

WE DO not have to create good. It is here now. We do not have to persuade God to be Love, or Life, or Truth, or Intelligence, for He is all these things already, and always has been. We do not have to ask Him to remember us, for He is always with us. We could not ask for any good that is not here already.

Neither do we have to fight evil. Fundamentally, evil is a false belief about good, and healing consists in unthinking the error by knowing the Truth. When you switch on the light in a room you do not have to chase the shadows out through the door or window. The light floods the room, and all is well, for darkness is not an entity; it is only the absence of light.

If we draw down the shades in every room in a house, that house will be in darkness, and is likely to become damp and unhealthy as well, no matter how brightly the sun may be shining outside. It we wanted to remedy this state of affairs, we would not try to make the sun shine more brightly (we could not), nor would we try to find a way to create sunshine inside. All we would have to do, indeed all we could do, would be to *raise the shades*. To raise the shades and open the windows would be the certain healing of that condition. The sun would pour in, and all the other benefits would follow.

God is with us at all times, but we close the windows of our soul and draw down heavy shades of fear, doubt, selfishness, etc., between Him and ourselves.

Salvation consists in raising these shades and opening the windows—then He does the rest.

GOD IS THE GREAT FRIEND

G OD is your best friend. God is always present, and
you can always turn to Him for help and guidance; and He never fails.

Of course it is foolish to think that God is just a very big man, a magnified edition of ourselves, but when people escape from this error they sometimes make the opposite mistake of thinking that God is only an impersonal force like electricity or gravity. This is the more dangerous mistake of the two, because it leaves people with no one to depend on but themselves, and that is the most tragic of all conditions. In such a case, people think, "I can overcome this difficulty if I get my thought right, but I have to do this alone and by my own power, and I may not be able to." They forget that God always helps.

Although God is not just a big man, *He has every quality of personality except its limitations.*

Think of God as a loving Father always ready to heal and comfort. Remember that God knows you and loves you and cares for you. Remember that He is and has infinite intelligence. Remember that He has all power, and that His nature is perfect divine love. Turn to Him today in exactly the same way and in the same spirit as you would have done when you were five or six years of age—but plus the larger understanding that you have since acquired.

A correct understanding of metaphysics cannot lessen your sense of the personal existence of God. It can only increase it. The Christ teaching comes not to destroy but to fulfil.

148

"Beloved, now are we the sons of God, and it doth not yet appear what we shall be: but we know that, when he shall appear, we shall be like him; for we shall see him as he is."*

* 1 John 3:2.

GOD'S OWN BILL OF RIGHTS

You can have anything in life that you are entitled to —if you will pay the price by building the mental equivalent for it. That is to say, you can get anything you are entitled to, provided that you make yourself mentally ready.

You have a right to anything that would be good for you—anything that would make you healthier, happier, more free, and more useful. This is God's Bill of Rights.

When you think, "I would like to do that, or be that, or have that," it is the voice of God in your soul which is telling you that the time has come to take a step forward.

Note particularly that you have a right only to the things which would be good for you and make you happy. Obviously you have no right to something that belongs to someone else, or to something which would infringe upon the rights of others, by making them do something which they would not want to do, for instance.

When you find yourself wanting something to which, in your heart, you know you are not entitled, it simply means that you are misinterpreting the channel. What you really want is the happiness and freedom that you think you would get by obtaining that particular thing —not really the thing itself which is only the channel.

In such a case, you should think, "That cannot be the way because I have no right to that, but there is some other way in which God can give me all that happiness and opportunity without infringing upon anyone else's rights."

Treat yourself by thinking, "I am in touch with the

Source of that good, and Divine Power is bringing it to me through another and legitimate avenue."

God's Bill of Rights says you have a right to health, happiness, and true success; and there is always a legitimate way to obtain these things. He will show you the path, and open it up if you trust in Him.

"In all thy ways acknowledge him, and he shall direct thy paths."*

* Proverbs 3:6.

MASTER, NOT SLAVE

ONE philosopher defined life as adaptation to environment. He said that anything that was alive would try to survive and, if possible, to grow, by adapting itself to the conditions in which it had to live.

There is of course a great deal of truth in this view as far as it concerns the plant and the animal world. Life is tenacious and extraordinarily resourceful in fitting itself to unsuitable conditions.

When we come to humanity, however, the case is altered. The Bible teaches us that man does not have to adapt himself to outer conditions as best he can, but that he has the power of changing or adapting outer things to fit him. This is the vital distinction between materialism and Spiritual Truth.

You do not have to make the best of unwelcome or unsuitable conditions, as a plant or animal does. You have within you the Divine Spark—the Indwelling Christ—and by awakening and developing this, your spiritual nature, *you can mould outer conditions to fit you.*

This process is Scientific Prayer. Through scientific prayer God, the Omnipotent, will work through you and make you the master of your destiny, the *master and not the obedient servant of outer things.*

Man differs fundamentally from even the highest animals because he has free will, the power of reason and intuition. By learning to use these faculties he gains his dominion. It is the Bible that says that God has given man dominion over all things.

GET SOME DEMONSTRATIONS

The royal road to progress in spiritual understanding is to solve *definite* problems by prayer.

Every time that you heal any condition, however small, by prayer, whether you are working for yourself or someone else, you gain an increase in spiritual understanding. One definite healing, whether it be of the body or of anything else, will teach you more about spiritual truth than hours of discussion or reading.

Do not waste time trying to answer theoretical or doctrinal questions.

Any such answer will be but another intellectual theory. Heal something, or treat yourself for divine understanding, and later on, when you are ready, you will find yourself really understanding the truth about the matter that puzzled you, instead of merely having a formal intellectual answer to it.

Do not expect to understand everything about God and man after a few weeks of study. Some questions in metaphysics which readily present themselves cannot really be answered without a good deal of preliminary preparation, and it is useless to try to answer them until this preliminary ground has been covered. It is useless for a student of algebra to try to understand the binomial theorem if he hardly yet understands a simple equation.

The way to get enough understanding to solve the more difficult problems is to do some practical healing, especially of your own difficulties. You always have enough understanding to meet any practical difficulty

that can come to you. You always have enough understanding to get freedom and harmony here and now
in the place where you are.

Jesus said, "By their fruits ye shall know them."*

* Matthew 7:20.

CAN HUMAN NATURE CHANGE?

SHALLOW thinkers sometimes pose the question, "Can human nature change?"

Or they say doggedly and pessimistically, "Human nature never changes," or, "Well, you can't change human nature."

The truth is that there is no need whatever for human nature to change. The nature of man is such that he can bring an unlimited quantity of either good or evil into his life and experience by using his mental faculties positively or negatively as the case may be. That is his nature, and no better arrangement could be imagined. Any change in it would be for the worse.

Note that people usually talk in the above strain when someone has been behaving badly—when he has been selfish, dishonest, or stupid. One never hears these remarks made in connection with a noble or wise action.

Sin, sickness, and death, wars and strife of every kind, come because man chooses to think negatively. He forgets God and thinks he himself is a material being; and an entirely separate person who must take care of himself at the expense of others, or else perish.

Now, however, the knowledge of the utter goodness and of the all power and all presence of God is rapidly spreading through the human race, and as men come to know this and realize it more and more, "human nature being what it is," conditions will improve in every respect until the whole race has freedom and harmony.

Human nature is such that man can turn to God anywhere at any time and, by believing in His care and protection, and thinking in accordance with this belief, fill his heart with peace and poise, rebuild his body into health and strength, and surround himself with harmonious and joyous conditions.

Human nature is such that when fear or temptation or anger or sadness or any other negative thing presents itself, man can melt it away by thinking rightly and regaining his happiness and confidence.

This is human nature as Providence has made it—and where is the point in discussing a change?

We have the key to perfect harmony and infinite perfection, and what more could we want?

"I am come that they might have life, and that they might have it more abundantly."*

* John 10:10.

NEVER hesitate to approach God in prayer because
you are not worthy. If you wait until you are
worthy you will never get near Him at all. If we had to
wait until we were worthy, no one would ever find salvation, because we cannot make ourselves worthy.

Turn to God just as you are; and however unworthy,
however sinful you may feel yourself to be, God will
help you and begin to make you worthy, as long as your
turning to Him is sincere and *wholehearted*.

Only God can improve us. Only God can cancel mistakes and rebuild our lives. The more sense of guilt we
may have the more reason is there for turning to Him.
God never refuses to help anyone. He comes when we
turn to Him; and He supplies whatever is lacking in us,
too.

The very fact that you are praying means that God
Himself has initiated the prayer, and what thought can
be greater than this? We are told that the Christ child
was born in a stable and not in a palace, and this is the
supreme symbol of the principle we have been considering.

"Ho, every one that thirsteth, come ye to the waters."*

* Isaiah 55:1.

GIVE IT TIME

PEOPLE sometimes accept the idea that a change of thought, plus turning to God in prayer, will transform their lives into harmony and freedom. The logic of this principle appeals to them, and they set to work upon it in earnest. Then, after a few days, they say, "Nothing has happened after all," and they drop back into their old negative thinking.

That is extremely foolish. The results of many years of general negative thinking are seldom corrected in a few days. No one who goes upon a new physical diet or medical regimen expects to reap the advantages in so short a time. You must keep up the new way of thinking for a reasonable period, and refuse to be discouraged by seeming failures at first.

The right motive for adopting right thinking is that it is right, and that wrong thinking is wrong; and we should do right whether it seems to pay dividends or not. Of course, it does pay dividends—fabulous dividends—but it usually takes a little perseverance in the face of preliminary slowness.

Beginners often get startling results at the outset, but not always; and we must not be dependent on such good fortune coming along. We must realize that right thinking and the Practice of the Presence of God are not matters of chance, but follow an unbreakable law, even if it takes a little time and perseverance to demonstrate that law.

"And ye shall seek me, and find me, when ye shall search for me with all your heart."*

* Jeremiah 29:13.

PLAIN AND SIMPLE

KEEP your prayers as simple as possible—simple in manner, and simple in thought. The secret of the successful prayer is that it is simple, direct, and spontaneous. As soon as a prayer becomes complicated, literary, or high flown, it has become an intellectual exercise and no longer has spiritual power.

In our metaphysical studies we should try to be equally simple and definite. We should make a point of expressing what we believe and understand in the simplest and plainest terms, both for our own sake and the sake of anyone we may be enlightening.

If your ideas about religion are expressed in a vague and involved style, if you use a lot of unusual or ambiguous words, it is a sure sign that you do not understand what you are talking about, and are trying to disguise the fact from yourself. This device is a well known trick of the subconscious to make us fool ourselves, and we should be on our guard against it.

Anything that you really understand you can explain in reasonably simple language—providing that it is susceptible of explanation at all. An air of heavy profundity conveyed in mysterious and vague phraseology is the hallmark of insincerity or of a muddled mind.

Do you remember the lines from the operetta "Patience"?

"And every one will say, as you walk your
    mystic way,
If this young man expresses himself in terms
    too deep for me,
Why, what a very singularly deep young man
    this deep young man must be!"

NOW

Has it ever occurred to you that the only time you ever have is the present moment? We have all heard this said many times but probably few of us realize, even slightly, all that it implies. It means that you can only live in the present. It means that you can only act in the present. It means that you can only experience in the present.

Above all, it means that *the only thing you have to heal is the present thought.* Get that right and the whole picture will change into one of harmony and joy. When some students hear this statement made they think, "Oh yes, I know that. I have known it for years"; but the chances are that they have not yet understood it thoroughly. When they do, remarkable results will follow.

All that you can know is your present thought, and all that you can experience is the outer expression of all the thoughts and beliefs that you are holding at the present time. What you call the past can only be your memory of the past. The seeming consequences of past events, be they good or bad, are still but the expression of your present state of mind (including, of course, the subconscious).

What you call the future, things that you may be planning, or things that you may be dreading—all this is still but a present state of mind.

This is the real meaning of the traditional phrase, *The Eternal Now.* The only joy you can experience is the joy you experience now. A happy memory is a present joy. The only pain you can experience is the pain of the present moment. Sad memories are present pain.

Get the present moment right. Realize peace, harmony, joy, good will, in the present moment. By dwelling upon these things and claiming them—and forgetting during the treatment, all other things—the past and future problems alike will take care of themselves.

"Finally, brethren, whatsoever things are true, whatsoever things are honest, whatsoever things are just, whatsoever things are pure, whatsoever things are lovely, whatsoever things are of good report; if there be any virtue, and if there be any praise, think on these things."*

* Philippians 4:8.

ONE WAY TO PRAY

THINK of God. Review some of the things that you know to be true about Him—His perfect goodness, infinite intelligence, all presence, limitless power, unbounded love, and so forth. Claim that God who is all those things, is with you—and believe it.

Read a few verses of Scripture or any spiritual book that helps you.

Claim that it is really God who is making this prayer through you—and believe it.

Say silently that you forgive everyone who may seem to need it; without exception or mental reservation—and mean it.

Ask God to forgive YOU for all mistakes you have ever made; and say you accept His forgiveness—and mean it.

Claim that God is now inspiring you, teaching you, and healing you. Claim that He is giving you the greatest of all gifts—HIMSELF—because, having Him, you will have everything else too. If there is any specific thing, great or small, troubling your life, claim that He will heal that—and believe it.

Give thanks for the privilege of visiting with God. Give thanks in advance for the peace of mind, the harmony, and the spiritual growth that this prayer is going to bring you—and mean it.

DON'T HURRY THE CHICKEN

A LITTLE city child was spending his vacation on a farm. They showed him a hen sitting on a nest of eggs, and told him that some day a little chicken would come out of each egg. The child was delighted at this dramatic idea, and every morning he went around expecting to see the miracle occur.

Days passed, and nothing happened. The eggs still looked exactly the same. Not the slightest change occurred in the appearance of things, and gradually his faith waned. At last one day he gave up hope altogether, and told himself bitterly that he had been deceived, and that nothing ever would happen.

Next day, however, from habit he went around to the nest as usual, but without any hope; and lo and behold, what was his joy to see a group of beautiful little chickens running about.

Of course wonderful changes had been taking place all the time, behind the shells, but there was nothing to show for it until the very last moment, when the little chicks suddenly emerged complete and perfect.

Some of our greatest demonstrations come to us like this. For a long time there is no change to be seen in the outer, but if we keep our faith strong, in spite of appearances, the demonstration will come—if at the 13th hour.

In this story it was the spectator who lost faith, and so it did not matter. If the mother hen had lost her faith —well, there would not have been any chickens. Give your demonstrations time to hatch. Keep your faith in God.

HOW PRAYER WORKS

PRAYER always helps, to the extent of our whole-heartedness and our faith; technically, we would say, to the extent of our understanding, or the height of consciousness attained. *According to our faith is it done unto us*, is the simplest and best way of stating it.

How prayer works is another question, and a very interesting one to students of psychology and metaphysics. This is what actually happens: Your prayer works by changing the subconscious part of your mind. It wipes out fear, and destroys the false ideas that have been causing the trouble.

Every condition in your life is the out-picturing of a belief in the subconscious. Every ailment, every difficulty that you have, is but the embodiment of a negative idea somewhere in your subconscious, which is actuated by a charge of fear. Prayer wipes out these negative thoughts and then their embodiment must disappear too. The healing must come.

Prayer, then, does not act directly on your body or on your circumstances; it changes your mentality—after which, of course, the outer picture must change too.

"And be not conformed to this world (the negative picture): but be ye transformed by the renewing of your mind, that ye may prove what is that good, and acceptable, and perfect, will of God."*

* Romans 12:2.

164

WHAT BECOMES OF EVIL?

WHAT is evil? You know that it is a false belief about God's perfect children or His perfect universe. A false belief has to be energized by a charge of fear or it can have no effect. A negative statement or suggestion that we do not believe, and therefore do not fear, cannot hurt us. All our troubles are caused by negative thoughts in the subconscious part of our own minds; every such thought consisting of a false belief and a charge of fear.

You all know that prayer heals by destroying evil, but sometimes people ask what becomes of the evil? Where does it go?

It is easy to understand the answer to this question when you know that any thought is but a vibration of the mind. Good thoughts are higher and finer vibrations, and negative thoughts are lower and grosser ones. The vibration is all there is of the thought. Prayer stops the mind vibrating at that particular point—it ends that vibration—and that is the end of the thing. You have doubtless seen and heard a tuning fork vibrating, thereby producing a certain note. Stop the vibration with your finger and the note ceases. What became of the vibration? It was only a movement and that movement has stopped. That is all.

If we are foolish enough to repeat the mistakes that caused our problem, if we again indulge in fear, criticism, self-pity, and so forth, we of course start a similar vibration and will have our trouble again; but it is not the old trouble "come back," it is a new copy that we have produced afresh.

165

There is no assurance of health and happiness except by training ourselves to think only harmonious thoughts. It is your *mental conduct* that determines the character of your life.

YOUR GREAT OPPORTUNITY

Your present problem is your great opportunity. Your own mind—The Secret Place, as Jesus called it—is the council chamber where the arrangements and decisions for your whole life are made; it is also the drafting room where the plans for your destiny are formed. Your life is your laboratory. The world is your workshop.

The only reason that you are here is that you may develop spiritually; and the only way to do that is to meet the many challenges of practical life and overcome them. You do not develop spiritually by running away from life into a hermit's cave or into some artificial, sheltered retreat, however good your intentions. Nor do you grow in spiritual stature by gaining your point through will power, brute force, or cunning deception.

You grow in grace and understanding by solving your daily problems as they arise, by the Practice of the Presence of God, by a tolerant attitude toward others, by plain horse sense (which is Divine Wisdom in you), by sincere and honest dealing at all times, and by cultivating a true sense of humor—which always brings us nearer to God.

The great point is that life is to be met and mastered. Outer conditions and appearances are simply of no importance in themselves except as they supply material for growth. It is the Law that any difficulties that can come to you at any time, no matter what they are, must be exactly what you need most at the moment, to enable you to take the next step forward by overcoming them. There need be no unqualified evils. The only real mis-

167

fortune, the only real tragedy, comes when we suffer without learning the lesson.

Doubtless everyone has felt at some time a desire to "get away from it all" to peace and quiet; has felt with a certain poet: "For me the sound of evening bells in ancient temples ringing." But that is not the way. You do not live in "an ancient temple," nor could you go to one now, even if it were the thing to do. Such thoughts are but sentimental dreaming. True peace comes not from outer conditions but from within. You can be filled with fear or hate on a remote mountain peak, and you can enjoy the Presence of God in the middle of Times Square.

Wake up! Realize God, and let Him give you perfect happiness and freedom here and now.

"I pray not that thou shouldest take them out of the world, but that thou shouldest keep them from the evil."*

* John 17:15.

BULB AND FLOWER

WHO HAS not at some time or other planted a bulb in the ground, or in a flower pot, and enjoyed the pleasure of waiting for the plant to appear and develop, and ultimately produce the glorious flower itself? For children, in particular, to have a bulb of their own (or several) and to feel that they are supervising its unfoldment in this way is one of the greatest thrills that life will ever give them.

Notice here that you naturally plant the bulb and expect the flower—the hyacinth or the crocus—to follow. No sane person would dream of planting the flower and expecting a bulb to come up; yet in our general life many of us do just that. We expect to begin with the flower and end with the bulb.

We think that we shall have desirable states of mind or body; happiness, freedom, health, if only we can change outer conditions in some way. Yet this is really trying to plant a flower and produce a bulb; because we are trying to put effect before cause.

The law of the universe is thought first, and then expression; and never can this law be reversed.

When you change your thought, or correct a false belief, you are planting the bulb of right thinking and you are certain to produce the flower of happiness and health. This is the way, and there is no other.

OUR LIFE'S ASSIGNMENT

THERE are certain Key Tasks in which we must attain at least some degree of mastery in this life, if we are not to waste our time. They are:

Making a personal contact with God.

Healing and regenerating our own bodies—demonstrating health.

Getting control of ourselves and finding our True Place.

Learning to handle other people both wisely and justly.

Perfecting a technique for getting direct personal inspiration for a general or a specific purpose.

Letting go of the past completely.

Planning the future definitely and intelligently.

To have made some real progress on each of these points, even though we may still be far short of mastery, is true success. Of course, we shall all advance farther in some of these directions than in others, but some progress must be made in each of them.

TAKING MATERIAL STEPS

WHEN you set out to solve a problem by means of prayer you should take all the ordinary normal steps in addition. Do not simply pray and then sit down and wait for something dramatic to happen. For instance, if you are praying for a position, you should pray for it as well as you know how each day, and then go out and visit agencies or prospective employers, write applications, or insert advertisements in suitable periodicals if that is customary in your line of work.

If you want a healing, treat about it in whatever way you usually find to be best and, in addition, take whatever material steps seem to be appropriate. Ask yourself if you are living in accordance with the laws of health, and if not, you must mend your ways at once.

If your business is not prospering, treat it, and then have a checkup to discover if you are managing it efficiently. If you find weak points in it, as you almost certainly will, you must correct them forthwith.

We certainly cannot expect to go on breaking the laws of the plane on which we live, and expect prayer to compensate for this foolishness.

When you treat for guidance or inspiration, it will often come in the form of your own common sense answer to the question. What we call "common sense" is just Divine Wisdom taking a particular form.

When we have no idea of what to do, then will be the time to treat for harmony or for guidance, and patiently await our answer, but all obvious and natural steps should always be taken.

CONTACTING GOD

TRUTH students are constantly told to contact God, to realize His Presence, to find God within themselves, to lean upon the Christ within; and so forth. Many people, however, are somewhat vague about the meaning of these phrases, and so it will be useful to consider exactly what they mean.

We cannot see God with our physical eyes, nor touch Him with our hands. Obviously, we can only contact Him in thought. But we do contact God whenever we think of Him. This is the meaning of the phrase to *find God within*. In the Bible, the word "within" means thought, and "without" or "outside" means the material world.

If we think quietly about God, by rehearsing the various things that we know about Him, we shall presently find that these truths are becoming more real to us, that they are no longer mere theories. This is *realization*, and realization is a matter of degree. These truths are felt more strongly at some times than at other times, and when we feel them more strongly we have a better realization and it has more power to heal.

The most important truth of all is that God is always with us, even though we are unaware of that fact, or forget it for the time being. To remind ourselves of His Presence, and to realize the fact to some extent, is to *find God within oneself*.

The Presence of God with us (in us) is sometimes called the Indwelling Christ or the *Christ within*, and to believe in our unity with it, and to have confidence in its saving, healing, and inspiring power, is to lean upon it.

172

To have faith that it will solve a particular problem is to *cast the burden* upon the Christ within.

"They shall call his name Emmanuel, which being interpreted, is, God with us."*

* Matthew 1:23.

SEEING GOD EVERYWHERE

THOSE on the spiritual path know that they should try to see God everywhere and at all times. Many people, however, are not clear as to what this really means.

The Truth of Being is that the whole creation is the self-expression of God. We ourselves are individualizations of Him, through which He seeks further and new expression.

Man does not understand this, and he forms false beliefs about the Truth. He sees limitation of all kinds around him. He feels himself to be separate from God, and dependent on his own efforts.

Seeing God everywhere means reminding ourselves of that truth. We should, of course, give our full attention to whatever we are doing at any time, but also hold the thought—"at the back of our minds," so to speak—that God is doing it through us. You can drive a car and watch the road carefully, and still, at the back of your mind, have the thought that you must make a telephone call when you arrive at your destination.

You should often remind yourself that God is really working through other people also; and especially during an important interview. If the other person is behaving badly, think that, rightly seen, God is working through him, and his conduct will change for the better.

One who is singing, or playing, or speaking in public, should hold the thought "God is healing the audience through me." This will help everyone in the audience, to some extent, and will make them friendly and appreciative.

This is the real Practice of the Presence of God.

TACKLING THAT BUGBEAR!

WHEN what seems an especially difficult problem, or a great emergency, presents itself, many students of Truth handle it in the wrong way. They start by thinking, "This is very serious," and then proceed to brace themselves mentally, so to speak, for a supreme effort; and plan to pray exceedingly "hard," or for a good many hours, in order to meet the difficulty.

All this is quite wrong. It simply builds up the problem into something far bigger than it was originally. Then they proceed to make a great mental effort to put power into the prayer. This again is quite wrong, because their mental power cannot do anything—only God can heal the condition—and this effort is really to affirm that He may not act.

The right attitude, the one that brings Victory, is:

1. To think "God can and will solve this problem if I adopt the right mental attitude."
2. Instead of speaking the Word from the low altitude of fear and limitation, and trusting to effort to magnify the Word; stop thinking of the problem altogether, and rise in consciousness. Take as long for this as may be necessary—a few seconds, a few minutes, or hours, or even days.
3. Having now attained a higher level—speak the Word gently *from that level*, and your problem will be solved.

We rise in consciousness by thinking about God, until we become really interested in Him. The altitude will vary with different people, as will the time needed to attain it, and these things will differ at different times for the same person.

Of course, this higher level of consciousness is not anything dreamy or abnormal. It is simply a healthy and rational interest in God.

THE UNFORGIVABLE SIN

THE Bible mentions the existence of an unforgivable sin, and this has greatly frightened innumerable Christians. From time to time I receive letters asking me what sin it is.

Let us be absolutely clear upon one point. There is no sin that a human being can commit that God will not forgive, upon sincere repentance.

The unforgivable sin is also spoken of as blasphemy against the Holy Ghost. In plain English this sin consists in shutting ourselves off from fresh inspiration or guidance from God. If your mind is already made up about everything appertaining to God; if you decide that you now know all the truth, and that you could not be mistaken; then it will not be possible for the Holy Ghost to open your eyes to error and lead you into higher truth—at least until you change your attitude.

Naturally, as long as this is your state of mind, no help or improvement can come to you; and in that sense only is it unforgivable—unforgivable while it lasts.

When you do change your attitude, enlightenment will come, and the sin will be destroyed.

In the Bible, this fact is stated in the dramatic manner of the oriental tradition; and does not imply what a literal interpretation would indicate.*

* See also, *The Sermon on the Mount*, pages 74 and 75.

A THRILLING EXPERIMENT

As a truth student you believe that God has all *power* and infinite *intelligence*, and that His nature is infinite *goodness* and *love*.

You also believe that He knows you, and loves and cares for you, and that in reality you are one with Him.

Why not make the following experiment, which will not only be thrillingly interesting, but will certainly bring some new and definite good into your life. It will also teach you more in one day than you could learn from books or lectures in many weeks.

Here is what you have to do. *For one whole day think, speak, and act, exactly as you would if you were absolutely convinced of the truth of the statements in the first paragraph.*

Of course you "believe" them theoretically, but to act in literal accordance with that belief is another matter. If this experiment is to mean anything you must positively act out the part.

To think in this manner all day will be the most difficult thing, because thought is so subtle. To speak in accordance with these truths will be easier; if you are vigilant. To act in accordance with them will be the easiest part, although it may require much in the way of moral courage.

If we believed in these truths with the same quiet unquestioning confidence with which we believe in the existence of, say, the subway or the telephone system, no problem, no grief, no fear, would stay with us very long.

MANY FORMS OF PRAYER

IT IS a mistake to think that there is only one form of prayer. There are many. As a rule, the best form is the one that happens to appeal most to you at the moment. The essential point in overcoming any difficulty, or solving any problem, is that you should become more conscious of the presence and the goodness of God than you are of the trouble; and as you approach this state of mind, any conscious fear that you have will steadily lessen.

Scientific prayer, or treatment, consists in getting the problem out of your mind by realizing the omnipresence of God, and it is by far the most efficient form of prayer —if you can use it.

Many people, of course, are not yet ready for this approach, and yet will get excellent results with orthodox forms of prayer, provided they dwell as little as possible upon negative things.

In praying for a sick person, for instance, avoid enumerating and dwelling upon the symptoms. Pray for healing and health. In praying for a soldier in battle, one should pray for his safety and welfare. Do not pray God to protect him from shot and shell or other dangers, as this is dwelling on the negative side. This mistake would not harm the soldier in any way, but it would very much lessen your power to help him. Pray Divine Love to be with him at all times, and have faith that this will be the case.

Truth students who employ scientific prayer, can use it in different forms. *The Golden Key* is best when you are confronted with a definite difficulty from which you want to be freed. When, on the other hand, you want to bring some new good into your life, a meditation like *The Good Shepherd*, might be better. Yet people get amazing results with any kind of problem by the use of either of these forms.

Just browsing at random through the Bible until the eye falls on an inspiring text has brought extraordinary results many times.

Pray gently. Don't make your prayers too long. Really expect results.

KNOWING THE TRUTH—
Not Manufacturing It

IT is important to remember that the Truth is true because it is true—not because we make it so. When we pray scientifically, we are reminding ourselves of and realizing better the Truth as it exists in reality.

Prayer does change things for us, but it changes them by tuning us in to the eternal Truth. It does not change the Truth itself. When we tune our radio into the right station we get the program that we want, but we do not change the program by so doing.

It is very helpful to remind yourself that the Truth is true whether you demonstrate it or not. If you were demonstrating one hundred per cent in every phase of your life, it would be delightful for you; but the Truth would not be any more true because of that. If you were not demonstrating at all, if you never could make a single demonstration in your whole life, the Truth would be just as true notwithstanding.

The law of Absolute Being is perfect eternal unchangeable harmony, and to believe this with some degree of conviction is the way out of difficulty.

You have nothing to deal with but your own thoughts, your own beliefs.

"And ye shall know the truth, and the truth shall make you free."*

* John 8:32.

GOD WORKS WITH JOY

Don't feel that you have to pray specifically for every good thing that you receive. Expect things to go right anyway, as the result of your general daily prayer.

Don't allow your metaphysical studies to cause you to lose interest in your general life, and especially in your business. When this happens, it may mean that you are trying to use metaphysics as an escape. If you are gaining an increase in true spiritual understanding, the quality of your day's work will improve, your interest in it will increase, and you will automatically move forward and upward to still more important things.

Don't pray or meditate as a duty. Realize that prayer is a visit with God and should be restful and joyous— not an unwelcome task.

Neither must you pursue your secular activities as necessary duties to be gotten over, that you may return to your metaphysical studies. You must perform them with joy for their own sake, remembering that, in the light of Truth, there are no secular activities, for all activities are spiritual, rightly seen.

You must have regular recreation or you will become stale. Recreation, also, is to be enjoyed for fun—as an expression of God—and not as a task to prepare yourself to pray better. An understanding joy in living is the highest prayer of all.

In Thy presence is fulness of joy.

SELF-CONDEMNATION KEEPS US BACK

PEOPLE who are honestly trying to follow the spiritual life often make the mistake of being too hard on themselves.

Because they do not seem to be progressing as fast as they would naturally like, or because they find themselves repeating some old fault which they thought they had completely overcome, or because after years in the teaching they catch a cold occasionally or have a minor accident, they feel discouraged, and condemn themselves mercilessly.

All this is foolish. If you are doing your best to use what Truth you know, at present, you are doing all that you have a right to expect of yourself. When one of these negative situations presents itself, quietly know the Truth about it, that is to say, *treat it*, and then treat your own sense of disappointment and discouragement, and believe that this prayer will be sufficient. Don't become tragic and make a fierce resolution to change all that. Such procedure would be using will power, and would really be building up the problem to many times its original size. Believe in your prayer.

Don't be impatient with yourself—but this does not mean that you are to be lazy or complacent. Handle yourself as a wise parent handles an obstreperous child—kindly, patiently, but with gentle firmness, not expecting too much too quickly, but foreseeing inevitable growth and improvement.

Of course, we know that there are people who refuse to recognize their faults and failures, and try to excuse themselves for anything—but such people are certainly not on the spiritual path.

Sincere students of Truth always tend in the other direction. We must remember that we owe Christian charity to ourselves as well as to others.

STUDY IS ONE THING—
Treatment Is Something Else

STUDYING metaphysics is one thing, but treatment is quite another. The rules for one cannot be applied to the other if success is to be attained. People often confuse these two things and consequently fail to demonstrate.

When you are studying—reading a metaphysical book, listening to a lecture, or thinking over the Truth that you know—you should be open-minded, wisely critical, taking nothing for granted, but weighing and considering, being as analytical as you please. You should not take someone's word for anything, but prove all things, holding fast to that which justifies itself by demonstrating. "By their fruits ye shall know them."*

When you are treating, the exact opposite policy is the right one. Then you must be dogmatic, insistent, arbitrary, cocksure, and mentally closed to anything but the Truth about the problem. You heal by knowing the Truth about the condition, and quietly refusing to recognize the reality of the error for a single moment. You must not in any way be tolerant toward it.

Do not analyze the condition that you want to heal; that is only flattering it with attention. Do not waste any time considering your doubts. Think, "God in me is stronger than all my doubts put together, so I shall not waste any time on them. The Truth is true at all times everywhere. The Truth is true about this apparent problem—and that is the end of the matter."

An electrical machine can be designed which will gen-

* Matthew 7:20.

185

erate current if it be driven mechanically, or do mechanical work as a motor if supplied with electric power instead. In the same way you can use your mental power for learning more Truth, or you can use it for applying the Truth you already possess; but these processes are still two different things.

God always works with intelligence and discrimination.

OMNIPRESENCE

I KNOW of no better way to name what we often call metaphysics, or the religion taught by Jesus Christ, than to call it the Practice of the Presence of God.

Intelligently understood, this includes the whole thing. Intelligently practised, it is the key to health, happiness, freedom, and spiritual progress.

It is utterly simple and it is powerful beyond human conception. It is this very simplicity that causes most people to miss it. It consists in, first believing, and then gradually realizing more and more that God is the only power and that everything we can be aware of is part of His self-expression. That is the whole story—simple but not, of course, easy, because we have lifelong habits of wrong thinking to overcome.

There could be no better nor more effective prayer than to sit down quietly and think over this greatest of all truths, which is the one whole and all inclusive Truth.

Do this quietly, without tension, as often as you feel is wise, even if it is only for a few moments at a time. You should not try to heal something by doing this— there are other times for healing work. Simply think about the Truth that God is the only Presence and the only Power. Think actively, turning the matter over in your mind and viewing it from many different angles. Do not strain for a realization, but simply think over this great Truth, and some of the innumerable consequences that must follow from the fact that it is true.

Enjoy reviewing the Truth, which is the nature of

God, *for its own sake*, and realization will come when you are not expecting it. As time goes on these realizations will become clearer and more frequent and you will find that outer conditions are steadily improving.

"Seek ye first the kingdom of God, and his righteousness; and all these things shall be added unto you."*

* Matthew 6:33.

DEMONSTRATION

IT IS an unbreakable spiritual law that whatever you understand you will express, or possess, or experience; and this law knows no exception.

This law works automatically, and requires no assistance from you, nor, on the other hand, could you prevent or even impede its action should you desire to do so.

As soon as you obtain a clear understanding of the Spiritual Truth about any desirable condition or object, it will automatically appear in your life. Naturally, you will see it coming through normal channels, or through a normal chain of circumstances; but those channels would not have opened and the necessary circumstances would not have occurred had you not obtained your understanding.

The solution of any problem, no matter what, cannot take longer than the time it takes to understand the Truth about it.

In the Old Testament the people were told that they could claim any land which they occupied or upon which they "put their foot." In the Bible, land always means manifestation, and spiritually the foot symbolizes understanding, and in psychology concentration.

The necessary understanding is, of course, to be obtained by prayer and meditation—the holy mountain.*

* See Isaiah 52:7 and Nahum 1:15.

189

Wᴇ ᴀʀᴇ all engaged in building our consciousness during every waking hour. This work is invisible, silent, and consequently overlooked by the bulk of mankind. Nevertheless, it is the most fundamental and the most far-reaching activity in life.

Everyone is building his consciousness all the time, little as he may suspect it. Hour by hour, and moment by moment, he is building good or evil, failure or success, happiness or suffering into his life by the thoughts that he thinks—the ideas that he harbors, the beliefs that he accepts, the scenes and events that he rehearses—in the hidden studio of the mind.

This fateful edifice, upon the construction of which you are perpetually engaged, is nothing less than your *self*—your personality, your identity on this earth, your very life-story as a human being.

If you are wise, if you are intelligent, if you exercise mere common sense, you will, in the light of what you know, build positively, constructively, which is to say *spiritually*.

That wondrous building, the spiritual consciousness, is called in the Bible, the Temple of Solomon, and we are told two wonderful things about that building. It was built in silence—without any noise,* and we know that thought is soundless; and it was built upon a rock†—and the Rock is the Christ truth of the Omnipresence and All-Power of God.

* i Kings 6:7.
† ii Chronicles 3:1.

190

A TREATMENT IS AN OPERATION

THE word "treatment" is usually applied to a prayer that is made to bring about a certain healing, or for some other specific purpose, as distinct from a general prayer, which is really a visit with God.

You must remember that a treatment is a definite practical action, having a definite object and a definite beginning and end. It is in fact a surgical operation on the soul.

Like a surgical operation, it must be conducted in a neat and methodical way, and under completely sterilized conditions.

Let us suppose that you decide to heal a certain difficulty by prayer. You know that your difficulty, whatever it is, must be caused by some negative thought or group of thoughts, charged with fear, and located in the subconscious mind; and that if you can wipe out these thoughts you will bring about the healing you seek.

You therefore turn to God, and remind yourself of His goodness, His limitless power, and His care for you. As you work the fear will begin to dissolve, and the recollection of these truths also corrects the erroneous beliefs themselves.

When you feel satisfied, or at least feel that you can do no more at that time, you thank God for the healing that you believe will come—and then you keep your thought off the whole matter until you feel led, after an interval, to treat again.

While you are treating you absolutely refuse to give any power to the difficulty or to admit for a moment that the healing will not come. This is the surgical cleanliness or sterilization.

General prayer is like the food and fresh air and exercise that keep us healthy, although we enjoy them for their own sakes. *A treatment is an operation.*

"He sent his word, and healed them."*

* Psalm 107:20.

WHAT IS "SEEKING THE KINGDOM"?

Seek ye first the kingdom of God, and his righteousness; and all these things shall be added unto you.—Matthew 6:33.

THE principle that Jesus expressed in these words is the basic law that underlies all demonstration or answer to prayer, for it is the realization of God that heals.

Many people know this in theory, but are confused about putting it into practice. Without quite realizing what they are doing they often think, "I will ignore this problem and think about God instead." Here there is a subtle mistake; because they are really thinking of their problem as existing in one place, of God as existing in another; and of themselves as going in thought from the first place to the second place.

This, of course, is by implication to reaffirm the existence of the problem in its own place, and such a belief will not heal.

What we have to do is to *seek the kingdom in the very place where the trouble seems to be*. We have to know that in Truth and reality it is not there, because God is there. This is the critical step. When we succeed in doing this, the difficulty disappears.

WORSHIP MEANS VICTORY

GOD is bigger than any problem.

God in you is greater than any difficulty that you, personally, can have to meet.

GOD cares for you more than it is possible for any human being to realize.

GOD can help you in proportion to the degree in which you worship him. You worship God by really putting your trust in Him instead of in outer conditions, or in fear, or in depression, or in seeming dangers, and so forth.

YOU worship God by recognizing His presence everywhere, in all people and conditions that you meet; and by praying regularly.

YOU deny Him when you allow fear to bluff you, when you think that limitation is inevitable, when you indulge in resentment or condemnation, or when you hold a grudge.

YOU pray well when you pray with joy; when you pray without effort, because you believe that God is making the prayer through you; and when you really expect the prayer to be answered—In God's way.

IS IT SELFISH?

Is IT selfish to pray for yourself? Some people think that it is, and say that you should pray only for others, but this, of course, is a foolish idea.

You must pray for yourself constantly. In fact, you should spend more time praying for yourself than for any other purpose.

How could it be otherwise? We worship God by believing in Him, trusting Him, and loving Him wholeheartedly—and we can attain to that only through prayer.

The sole object of our being here is that we may grow like Him—and we can do that only through prayer.

It is impossible to make any spiritual progress unless we are trying to lead the Christ life—and we can do that only through prayer.

Spiritual progress must be slow as long as we are worried, frightened, resentful, sick, or discouraged—and those things can be overcome only through prayer.

It is a duty and a joy to help others, wisely, and to leave the world a better place than we found it—and we can do that only through prayer.

The more we pray for ourselves the more power will our prayers have for any other purpose whatever; so we see that praying for ourselves is the reverse of selfishness—it is truly glorifying God.

ACTUALIZING THE VISION

THE history of the salvation of an individual could be summarized in this way: First he sees the vision; and then he actualizes it.

Now what does seeing the vision, in this sense, really mean? Does it mean some wonderful, mystical experience, such as those of which some of the Bible prophets speak? Certainly not. If such a thing were necessary, then obviously the vast bulk of mankind would have no chance of salvation.

You "see the vision," in this sense, whenever you experience a desire to be a better Christian, to gain more knowledge of God, to get a healing for the body, or to solve any kind of practical problem through prayer.

That is the vision. You desire to be something finer and greater than your present self, and you believe that prayer can bring this about. Or, you desire to overcome some difficulty, or to escape from some limitation, and you believe that prayer can bring that about. That is the vision.

The vision is the conviction that God saves and heals; and now, having seen the vision, the next step is to actualize it—to make it actual in your life.

That is done by reorganizing your life—your thoughts, your words, your deeds—to bring it into harmony with what you know to be the Law of God. That is the Practice of the Presence of God that we so often speak of, and it cannot fail.

MENTAL DRUDGERY IS NOT PRAYER

EXPECT more from your prayers than perhaps you have been accustomed to. The power of your prayer depends upon the amount of faith that you yourself have in it. To pray in the spirit that "even if this prayer does not do any good at least it cannot do any harm," is not, really, to pray at all.

Long sessions of prayer are usually a mistake. Have enough faith in the love of God to believe that a short heartfelt prayer is just as good as a long one; and indeed it is. Of course the short prayer can be repeated at intervals.

Too long a session of prayer usually means that in your heart you really doubt the love of God, and think that a great deal of effort and toil will be necessary to move Him. That is actually a subtle way of using will power.

People say, "I prayed long and hard because I wanted to raise my consciousness." Well, of course, no object could be more important than that, and if this were the way to do it, you would have acted wisely—but it is not.

That kind of thing does not raise your consciousness an atom. It tires and discourages you. You are trying to *force* an immediate realization, and that proceeding is doomed to failure.

Pray quietly and sincerely for a reasonable time—and then leave it, expecting success. Then do something quite different. Read a good secular book or magazine, or attend to general business, or go to bed if it is night time; and a beautiful demonstration will arrive at the proper season.

THE GOLD, AND THE SILVER, THE IVORY, THE APES, AND THE PEACOCKS

W E KNOW that the spiritual consciousness which we are all engaged in building, is spoken of in the Bible as the Temple of Solomon. The name Solomon, literally, means peaceful, and in the Bible symbolizes wisdom. This is logical, for peace of mind is the foundation of all spiritual building, of happiness, and of all lasting success in any field. Indeed, peace of mind may be called the hallmark of understanding. To seek peace and pursue it,* is supreme wisdom, since it insures the building of the temple.

The Bible states that five things were to be found around the temple—*gold, and silver, ivory, and apes, and peacocks.*† This is the scriptural manner of telling us that there are five principal temptations that may come to the soul that is striving to be free—striving to build the spiritual temple. The particular form that each temptation will take will naturally vary according to the temperament and circumstances of the subject, but in principle will be the same for all.

First comes the *gold*, and this stands for the desire for personal power over other people, the desire to regulate their lives, to make them toe the line—our line, naturally—and even to make use of them. Many people on the spiritual path have given way to this temptation. They must dominate other people's souls. They tell themselves that it is done for the good of the victims, of course, but it is really a craving for personal power and

* Psalm 34:14.
† 1 Kings 10:22.

198

glorification. It is not an ignoble sin like that connected with the silver, but for that very reason it is a deadly one, and far more dangerous and far-reaching and enduring. It is spoken of elsewhere in the Bible as the "scarlet woman of Babylon."

The true meaning of gold, the thing that gold symbolizes when rightly understood, is the omnipresence and availability of God; and of course religious tyranny is a denial of this. You should do all you can to help, to enlighten, and to inspire others, as far as your own understanding will permit, but you must never try to coerce their souls, to dictate their convictions; or to hold them to yourself, or to your own opinions. Religious tyranny is poisonous to the victims; but it is absolutely mortal to the tyrant.

Next comes the *silver*. This stands for greed of money or money's worth, for material objects that can be bought, and even for riches themselves by the mere possession of a large fortune. Or it may be that the offender is not interested in riches. What he wants is to occupy a position of honor and dignity in the eyes of the world. He wants to be "somebody." He wants to be considered important and to have adulation or applause.

Often he wants to be a "leader," not because he has a message to give—in such cases he never has—but to be important and looked up to. He is like the girl who wants to be a prima donna, not because she has a voice and longs to use it—and is willing to work hard and equip herself—but simply to be in the newspapers and to receive the applause and the bouquets.

He does not care for power. He is not profound enough to fall into that sin. He is satisfied with the appearance of power and distinction. He is the victim of vanity and egotism.

Now this is, plainly put, to worship the world instead of God, and the natural result is obvious. This sin is a base and ignoble one, readily detected even by thoughtless people, and therefore is not very dangerous, except to the culprit himself. For him it is an insurmountable barrier across the spiritual path until it is recognized and removed.

Next comes the *ivory*. This stands for undue attachment to a particular teacher, a particular textbook, or a particular church or other organization. It is a mistaken loyalty. It is an unselfish error, but a deadly one. Any religious teacher or writer, however eminent, any church or center, however much beloved, is still but *a means to an end*. The end itself is spiritual growth.

Many students derive great help from a certain teacher or a certain church, and make much progress, for a time. Then they find that they have outgrown that teacher, and could get more help elsewhere, but they refuse to move—from a mistaken sense of loyalty.

You positively owe no loyalty to anyone or anything but your own soul—and that is the most sacred loyalty you could have. Recognize with gratitude all the help that you receive from any source, but remember that your loyalty is due to God, through your own spiritual development. You must feel free at any time to go wherever you get the most help, irrespective of personal considerations. To do otherwise is to commit the sin against the Holy Ghost.

The *ape* stands for bodily temptations such as sensuality, addiction to drink, drugs, and so forth. These things are so obvious that the victim cannot deceive himself about them, so that at least he knows where he stands. They can, of course, be overcome by systematic prayer.

The *peacock* stands for vanity. It may take the form of intellectual pride, or of a snobbish idea that a small and obscure group cannot have anything worth while to give, or the desire to stand in with what is fashionable and powerful even though it be erroneous.

It also includes spiritual pride on the part of those who really are in Truth, and this is worse than any of the other forms.

PRAYER ALWAYS THE ANSWER

PRAYER is always the solution. No matter what kind of difficulty may be facing you, no matter how complicated your problem may seem—prayer can solve it and re-arrange everything beautifully. Of course you will also take whatever practical steps seem to be indicated, and if you do not know what steps to take, prayer will show you.

Prayer will bring any good thing into your life, and it will find its own ways and means to do so. Prayer is constantly bringing about the seemingly impossible, and there is no conceivable problem that has not at some time been solved by prayer.

When we remember that God really is omnipotent, untrammeled by what we call time or space or matter, or the vagaries of human nature, it is easy to see that there can be no limit to the power of prayer.

Even if you feel very strongly about some condition you must not be tempted to say "It is useless to pray about this because I am determined to take such and such an action tomorrow, in any case." Pray about it, nevertheless, and when tomorrow comes it will still be open to you to do whatever you wish. But, you may think better of it after you have prayed.

You can pray about a problem and solve it at any stage, but of course the earlier you tackle it the easier will your work be.

THE SPIRITUAL BASIS

One is either on the Spiritual Basis or he is not, for there is no half way house in this.

You are on the Spiritual Basis:—

If you definitely give all power to God, in the most literal, practical, and matter of fact sense of the phrase; and no power to conditions existing at any time.

If you refuse to give power to error by fearing it.

If you really believe that prayer can and will do anything.

If you really believe that your happiness and well-being are vitally important in the eyes of God.

If you realize that whatever ideas and beliefs you accept *must* be expressed in your body, in your surroundings, and in all your relationships and activities.

If you try to see the Presence of God everywhere.

If you realize that fundamentally you have nothing to deal with but your own thoughts.

If, in short, you understand that you are in a mental universe, that things are thoughts, and that one's life history is fundamentally the expression of his belief about God.

WHEN GOD DOES NOT ACT

W_{E ALL} believe that the love of God is invincible. We all believe that His intelligence, His knowledge, and His power are infinite. We all believe that God cares for us to a degree beyond imagining, and that each one of us is equally precious in His sight. Yet, in many cases healing and harmony do not follow from this knowledge. Why is this?

In most cases it is because we have forgotten that these qualities have to be embodied in ourselves before they can appear in our lives. To know of them as existing in God is not sufficient. We must be seeking to express them in our personal lives before they can do anything for us.

Divine Love will be all powerful to heal and help us in so far as we are expressing Divine Love in our own thoughts, words, and deeds. Divine Wisdom will be able to guide us in so far as we pray for guidance and are honestly prepared to do God's will, and are trying to live the Christ life. Divine Power will be potent in our lives to the extent of the faith that we have in it.

The only way to know God is to seek to express Him in our lives.

THE CONSECRATED LIFE

O F WHAT does the consecrated life consist?
Your life is a consecrated one when you are ready at all times to do the will of God—when you are willing and anxious that God may be fully expressed through you; through your thoughts, words, and deeds, during every hour of the day.

If you are earnestly trying to live in this way, you have consecrated your life to God, and you can do no more.

You are not concerned with the question of results. Results belong to God.

Whether you are seen as doing something remarkable or even magnificent in the outer, or whether your external activities seem to be insignificant, is of no importance. You are consecrating your life to God and you can do nothing greater, finer, or higher than that.

"Here am I; send me."*

* Isaiah 6:8.

DON'T USE A STEAM HAMMER TO KILL FLIES

Don't kill flies with a steam hammer. That way is cumbersome and expensive. A great power-hammer costs a lot of money and takes up a great deal of room. In fact, erecting it and then operating it will occupy most of your time. Then you will have to catch each fly separately and stick it in place while the huge hammer does its work.

By far the best way to kill flies is to buy a fly swatter at the five and ten, and hit the fly once, when it appears. This is simple and takes only a moment out of your life.

Of course, all this is just a way of saying that many people have an unfortunate talent for doing things the hard way when there is an easy way quite handy. They spend half a day running around to accomplish something that another person would do quietly in half an hour or less, by acting intelligently. They write and re-write a long letter half a dozen times, when fifty words on a postcard, or five minutes on the telephone, would have settled the matter easily. They must always go from New York to Jersey via Europe, India and China. In the words of the Chinese fable, they burn down the house to get a piece of roast pork.

You should accustom yourself to doing things as simply, directly, and with as little fuss as possible, particularly in your spiritual life. When you pray, come to the point. Don't hover over the problem, but swoop at it. Know the Truth without preliminaries or beating about the bush.

In other words, do not use a steam hammer to kill flies.

WHY SHOULD THIS HAPPEN TO ME?

WHEN a difficulty arises, people sometimes ask, "What have I done to deserve this? Why should this happen to me? I am not aware of having done anything very wrong."

The answer to this is that our experience is the resultant of the totality of our beliefs, and that we all have many beliefs and ideas that we do not know about, hidden away in the subconscious, things that we have read or were told in childhood, or since. Also, beliefs and tendencies with which we were born are still with us and have power to influence our lives.

Everyone has some of these things and when they express themselves in the form of trouble it means that the time has come to clear them out, by overcoming that trouble, whatever it is, with prayer and wise action.

Your general daily prayers and meditations, your reading of spiritual books, are carrying on this cleansing work all the time.

Quite often your difficulties are due not to something out of the past but to some mistake you are making in the present time. You are probably not doing anything usually considered wrong, but you may be overworking (which is using will power), you may be neglecting the ordinary rules of health, or you may be cutting down your prayer time under the delusion of being "too busy." *Too busy to have time for God!*

Have a brief stock taking and if the weak point is not apparent, ask God to show it to you.

He careth for you.

PRAYER AND WISE ACTION

IN SOLVING a problem by prayer it is usually necessary to take certain practical steps as well. Wise action must be added to prayer. Pray about your difficulty but also claim Divine Guidance, and then take any steps that common sense dictates. We cannot remind ourselves too often that what we call common sense is itself an expression of Divine Wisdom. It is foolish to pray for help while neglecting some obvious and handy stepping-stone.

Many people seem to have the idea that taking some "material" step shows a lack of faith in God and lessens the power of the prayer. They ask if that is not trying to serve two masters.

The exact contrary is the case. We all know that an action is but the outer expression of a thought, and that a wise action is the expression of a wise or true thought, and so to take wise steps is but the proof that one is thinking rightly, and is, indeed, a part of the prayer itself.

We must learn to see God in our words and our deeds, as well as in our thoughts.

ALL KNIFE AND NOTHING TO CUT

How can you progress rapidly in the knowledge of Truth? What is the best way to grow spiritually? How can you acquire power in prayer?

The answer to these three questions is this: Use all the understanding that you have at the present moment to overcome your present difficulties, whatever they may be.

How can you get a better knowledge of God? How can you get to know God? Again, the answer is the same, use whatever understanding you have at the present time to solve practical problems. Every problem solved by prayer, every difficulty that you overcome by spiritual treatment, teaches you more about God and develops your spiritual nature faster than anything else could possibly do. One difficulty conquered in this way teaches you more than the best teacher, or the best book.

People sometimes ask, "How can I learn to love God?" The answer is still the same. Overcome a difficulty, great or small, by prayer, and you will feel a sense of thankfulness and joy which is really love for God, and once this begins, it will grow and grow, until it dominates your whole life.

What is the use of studying Truth, of reading books, and attending lectures, if you do not use the thing in practice. It seems strange, and yet it happens, that there are people who study metaphysics for years and actually never try once to put it to use. It is no wonder that they make practically no progress. In such a case, there is no balance between intake and output which is essential for every living thing. It is all knife and nothing to cut.

God will not give us more unless we use what we already have.

LEAVING THINGS IN GOD'S HANDS

PEOPLE sometimes speak of leaving a problem in God's hands. Of course this is an excellent thing to do, and especially where it seems that there is nothing else that can be done about it.

You should be careful, however, that you know the true meaning of this phrase. To leave a thing in God's hands does not mean simply to hand it over to God, and then forget all about it; or, what is worse, to permit ourselves to think negatively about it from time to time.

It means that every time the subject comes to mind you must affirm that God is solving the problem in His own good way, and that all will be well. If you follow this policy the demonstration will come sooner or later.

The way to treat a bulb is to put it in the ground in a suitable place, where it will have the right kind of soil and enough moisture, and, later on when it is ready, plenty of sunshine too. That is working in harmony with the laws of nature.

To throw it into a drawer and forget about it is a different thing altogether. That is not leaving it to nature, but the contrary. The first policy is creative, the other is not.

So it is with your problems. Leaving them in God's hands is a living, creative spiritual activity.

"Be still, and know that I am God."*

* Psalm 46:10.

211

NEW NAMES FOR OLD THINGS

MODERN psychology has done good work in throwing new light on many aspects of the human mind, and thus helping us to understand ourselves better. Naturally, it cannot take the place of prayer, but still it has its uses.

We need to know something of how the human mind works in order that we may redeem it. It is well, however, to remember that we have always known a good deal about it in general; and we should avoid being confused or intimidated by modern psychological terminology. For the most part, this is but giving new names to old things. The new names are often more precise and instructive, but the things they refer to are things that we have always known about.

We have always known, for instance, that at any given time we are conscious only of a certain number of ideas, of the things that we are doing and thinking about at the moment—and these represent what psychology calls "the conscious mind."

We have always been aware that we know a great many things about which we are not thinking at any given time, some of which we have completely forgotten, but which might be brought back by some unexpected incident; and this is what psychology calls "the subconscious or unconscious mind."

We have always known that we have a tendency to fool ourselves by thinking that we act from one motive when the fact is that we are acting from quite a different one; and this is "rationalization."

We have always known that human nature is very ingenious in inventing some illicit scheme to evade an unpleasant duty or to avoid facing up to an unwelcome fact—and this is "the escape mechanism."

And so on with most of the technical terms of present-day psychology. The important thing is to make sure that when we use them they are our servants and not our masters.

Of course, the one thing that matters is to get a better knowledge of God, and of ourselves, and any study and any experience that helps toward that end is good.

"Acquaint now thyself with Him, and be at peace."*

* Job 22:21.

JUST WHAT TO DO

IF a new problem arises . . .
Get back to basic principles.

If an old problem continues to stick . . .
Get back to basic principles.

If everything seems to be sticking . . .
Get back to basic principles.

If you feel depressed or discouraged . . .
Get back to basic principles.

If you find yourself nervous, or even frightened . . .
Get back to basic principles.

If someone is being troublesome . . .
Get back to basic principles.

If you want to make faster progress than you seem to be doing . . .
Get back to basic principles.

PRAYER DOES IT

WHATEVER your problem may be, prayer can solve it for you. Whatever your burden may be, prayer can melt it away. Whatever you may lack to make your life complete, prayer can supply.

Remember that you are praying whenever you are thinking of God—whether you call it prayer or not. You are praying whenever you are reading the Bible or any spiritual book, when you are meditating, and whenever you claim that God is thinking, speaking, or acting through you.

Thus you see that whenever you are doing any of those things, you are overcoming; you are drawing nearer to God. You are spiritualizing your nature; you are, in the modern phrase, cleaning out the subconscious.

People often ask what is the best way to redeem the subconscious mind, to get rid of the fear and other negative things that are to be found in it. Again the answer is—*prayer*. The best way to redeem the subconscious is to meet each difficulty as it arrives—by prayer —and to rejoice in this knowledge that the Practice of the Presence of God is the great deliverer. It is by far the best and most powerful form of psychiatry.

MERCY AND TRUTH

"MERCY and truth are met together; righteousness and peace have kissed each other."*

This verse states a great spiritual law. It say that *mercy* and *truth* are met together. That means, of course, that when we find ourselves in a difficulty, our salvation consists in knowing the Truth about it. When we realize the Truth, even to a small extent, the condition begins to heal, and this is the "mercy" that we receive. Truth is the healer, and therefore the agent of mercy.

The second half of the verse says, in an oriental figure of speech, *righteousness* and *peace* have kissed each other. Righteousness, as we know, really means right thinking, and the lesson here is that right thinking brings peace— that they go together. Peace of mind is the first and greatest gift that a human being can receive, and it is only to be obtained by the realization of truth.

Peace of mind is not only the greatest blessing in itself, but it brings many other prizes into our lives. For instance, peace of mind sets energy free in the subconscious, and enables us to do many things which otherwise would be beyond us. It heals the body; it allows new ideas to come through from Divine Mind; and, indeed, it may be said to be the hallmark of understanding.

* Psalm 85:10.

THE UNEXPECTEDNESS OF GOD

ONE of the most wonderful things about God, from the human point of view, is His unexpectedness. When we pray in the true spiritual manner, leaving the solution to Him, and desiring only that His will may be done—because we know that the Will of God is always something joyous and good—we know that our prayer will be answered, but we never know just how.

God answers prayer in the most unexpected way; and that is half the fun. When we pray it usually seems that there is some obvious way in which the demonstration will come—and then, lo and behold, it comes in a surprising and delightful way. Sometimes it seems that there is no way, humanly speaking, in which the problem can be solved, and yet solved it is, and in some glorious and thrilling manner.

God acts out of the blue, so to speak. If we would only have a quiet faith in our prayer, without being tense or fussing, leaving ways and means to Him, but being confident that the demonstration will come, come it will, and the result will always be even better than we hoped.

"Delight thyself also in the Lord; and He shall give thee the desires of thine heart."*

* Psalm 37:4.

AN AMAZING BOOK

WHICH is by far the greatest of all books?—The Bible.

Which is the most widely circulated of all books; the world's all time best seller?—The Bible.

Which has been the most loved of all books?—The Bible.

Which of all books has been the most hated (by a small minority who did not understand it)?—The Bible.

Which is the most thrillingly interesting of all books? —The Bible.

Which is the best, clearest, and most useful book on practical psychology?—The Bible.

Which is the simplest and most effective textbook on metaphysics?—The Bible.

Which is the greatest of all story books?—The Bible.

What book contains the world's greatest and finest poetry?—The Bible.

Which is the world's best collection of well written, instructive, and inspiring biographies?—The Bible.

What book can one study to get a good command of forceful, convincing, and beautiful English?—The Bible.

Is there a short cut to the spiritual life?—Yes, The Bible.

Which is the one book that no one anywhere can afford to neglect?—The Bible.

SO YOU BELIEVE THAT

W<small>E ARE</small> all constantly exposed to negative suggestions as we go through life. Well meaning
people give them to us in conversation. We hear them
or overhear them at social gatherings, business meetings,
and so forth, and we meet them in the newspapers and
on the radio. This fact worries many people, and they
almost wish that they could shut themselves up in a
high tower where nothing negative could penetrate.

Of course such an idea is quite erroneous. We are in
this world just to learn to handle this very problem,
and it would be a capital mistake to run away from it,
even if that course were practicable. We are here to
learn the lesson that evil has no power except that which
we give it by believing in it.

No negative thought or false suggestion can do you
the slightest harm unless you *accept* it. And remember,
that to receive a negative suggestion, and to *accept* it,
are two utterly different things. Unless you *accept* an
idea it does not exist as far as you are concerned, for it
has no effect in your life.

Naturally, this is just as true for positive or good
ideas as it is for negative ones. If you do not *accept* a
good or true idea it cannot influence you. For centuries
people have read in the Scriptures that God is love and
that faith moves mountains, but they have still been
frightened and frustrated notwithstanding—because they
did not really *accept* these ideas, although they gave a
formal assent to them out of respect for the Bible.

Now the vital question presents itself: What do I
mean by *accepting* an idea? *How* does one *accept* an

idea? Well, it is quite simple. To *accept* an idea, is to *believe* it; that is all.

If you believe a negative suggestion, it hurts you to the extent of your belief. If you do not believe it, it cannot hurt you. If, for instance you hear someone say that Chicago is in Texas, you do not believe it, and so when you write to people in that city your letters do not go astray. And the same thing applies to good ideas.

The Gospel is the Good News but it cannot help you unless you *accept* it or *believe* it—and, of course, if you do believe it you are trying to live it.

"Acquaint now thyself with him, and be at peace: thereby good shall come unto thee."*

* Job 22:21.

MY HOLY MOUNTAIN

*They shall not hurt nor destroy in all my holy mountain.—Isaiah
11:9.*

GOD has promised that any one of us who really
desires it, and means business, can have peace of
mind, poise, and security, and with these things go
naturally freedom, all round harmony, and a joyous
and interesting life.

God has promised us that, if we really desire it, and
mean business, we can live in perfect safety no matter
what may be happening around us; and that we shall
not only be safe but that we shall realize it and thus be
free from even groundless fear. And because God is
Divine Love He has ordained that we can produce these
conditions, at least to a large extent, for those we love
and wish to help. So this is not just a selfish arrangement
for taking care of ourselves exclusively.

God makes this glorious promise in the pages of the
Bible, in many different texts throughout the whole
book; each worded differently and approaching the subject from a different angle, but teaching the same lesson.

The gist of the matter is that to bring these things
about we have to pray frequently, to try to get as good
a realization of the Presence of God with us, as we can,
and to train ourselves to give all power to Him—which,
of course, means giving no power to anything unlike
Him.

It is needless to say that this condition is not completely attained overnight. It takes time. But it is surprising how much can be attained, and how one's con-

221

ditions can be radically improved for the better even in a few weeks—if he means business.

This, of course, is really what some of the old mystics called the Practice of the Presence of God.

The important thing is to know that it is not something mystical, abstract, intricate; but something plain, simple, and practical, if not exactly easy.

Remind yourself frequently throughout the day that God is with you, caring for you, and guiding you; and that whatever you are saying or doing is really being done through you by Him. Not very subtle or abstruse, is it?

You know that, in the Bible, the mountain always means uplifted thought, awareness of the Presence of God, and is therefore holy—which means not pious or sanctimonious, but peaceful, healthful, harmonious, and joyous.

The promise is clear and unmistakable. We cannot be hurt in any way if we dwell, much of our time, on the holy mountain.

ROUGH ROAD

EVERYONE on the spiritual path has found that it happens occasionally in the early years—and not often then—that he suddenly finds himself almost or quite unable to pray. Often it seems that he cannot get any sense at all of contact with God. This naturally depresses him and sometimes leads to greater fear and almost to despair.

Now, these severe reactions are not necessary, once you know that everyone goes through them. If you think that you are the only one who has ever experienced these things they will naturally frighten you; but now you know that such is not the case.

This trouble is caused by overdoing. You have been praying too long or too hard, or you have been giving too much time to spiritual work exclusively, instead of having other interests in your life too. It is really a condition of staleness and psychological congestion. The medieval mystics called these times "seasons of dryness" and suffered severely because they believed them to be sinful.

The remedy is not to struggle, but to know that this will surely pass, and your spiritual joy return. If you cannot pray, do not try, but think, "God is so good that I need not pray; He will take care of me anyway." (Of course, this itself is a wonderful prayer.) If there is a feeling of depression, think, "me" is depressed, but "I" am not. I know better.

On a long motor tour, it sometimes happens that you come upon a piece of rough, bad road. For hundreds of miles the going has been perfect, but now you are shaken and bumped badly, but you do not worry, because you know for certain that it will only last for a few miles. Indeed, there is probably a notice saying "Pavement ahead" three miles or seven miles or what not.

If the road gets rough in your spiritual life, then turn toward the light and say "pavement ahead."

"Be still, and know that I am God."*

* Psalm 46:10.

A THIEF IN THE NIGHT

IT is no use struggling for a realization. You cannot compel it by will power, and this very struggling actually postpones it. The proper thing to do is to pray quietly as well as you can, knowing the Truth as clearly as you can, because it is the Truth and you have long since decided to stand for Truth. When you do this you have done your duty and you know that since no word of prayer can be wasted or be void it must demonstrate at some time. Do not be impatient.

Praying in this way, a realization will come when you least expect it; perhaps while you are praying, perhaps later when you are preoccupied with other things. Meanwhile, remember that you can get wonderful demonstrations without any conscious realization at all, although of course a realization is to be desired because it signifies a longer step in advance.

Jesus, in his graphic and fearless way compares this experience—surprisingly enough—to the entry of a thief or burglar into a house in the middle of the night. Lesser souls would have been too timid to use such a comparison, but Jesus desired to arouse the attention and drive the lesson home by a particularly striking and dramatic figure of speech. It is obvious that the burglar will choose a time when he is not likely to be expected. The one thing he desires is that the householder shall not be prepared. The essence of his work is surprise.

Now, this is just how realization comes, and I think that after considering this very vivid picture we are never likely again to work directly for a realization.

"Watch therefore: for ye know not what hour your

Lord doth come. But know this, that if the goodman of the house had known in what watch the thief would come, he would have watched, and would not have suffered his house to be broken up. Therefore be ye also ready: for in such an hour as ye think not the Son of man cometh."*

* Matthew 24:42-44.

HOW MUCH FAITH IS NECESSARY?

Have faith in your own faith. Have faith enough in yourself to believe that you really have enough faith to move mountains.

Is this a strange idea? Probably it is for many people, yet Jesus taught it.

People are constantly saying that they wish they had more faith because if they had they could get better results. You have to realize, however, that this attitude of mind is extremely negative, and must hold you back. It is affirming, although indirectly, that your faith is very poor—and you know what that means.

Jesus said that the very smallest amount of faith (like a grain of mustard seed) is sufficient.

If you have faith enough to pray at all, you have enough faith to start with. If you had no faith, you would not be praying.

Have faith in your own faith, and that in itself will build it up more and more until the work is done.

"Be not faithless, but believing."*

* John 20:27.

WHAT METAPHYSICS IS NOT

METAPHYSICS is not Pollyanna. It does not say that "everything will be all right." Things will not be all right unless you make them so by right thinking. Definitely you can bring any amount of trouble on yourself by wrong thinking, and neglect of God.

It is not a *get rich quick* scheme. It teaches that if you have faith in God, He will supply your needs bountifully; but metaphysics will not bring money for its own sake.

It does not teach that you have only to *order what you want*—by thinking it—and that God must obey your orders. This absurd idea usually ends in disaster. The truth is that you can demonstrate only what you really have the consciousness for; and what you have the consciousness for you must demonstrate.

It is not *mind over matter*. It teaches that what we see around us is but our own thoughts and beliefs objectified. Thus we do not try to dominate something outside of our minds, but to change our minds.

It does not pretend that your *trouble is imaginary*. It admits that it is there as an experience; but it says that that experience can be dissolved by realizing the Presence of God.

It is not *faith healing* in the ordinary sense of fighting a supposedly real evil with blind faith and will power. It teaches an intelligent and understanding Faith based on the goodness and all-presence of God.

It is not *Pantheism*. Pantheism, as generally understood, gives the outer world a separate and substantial existence and says that it is part of God—including all

the evil and cruelty to be found in it. The truth is that
God is the only Presence and the only Power, that He
is entirely good, that evil is a false belief about the
Truth; and that the outer world is the out-picturing of
our own minds.

THE POWER OF THOUGHT

The Laws of Thought are the Laws of Destiny. *Whatever you believe with feeling, that you bring into your life.*

These little essays are intended to instruct the reader in Basic Spiritual Truth, and to furnish material for short meditations. They were published once a week over a number of years.

The subjects are usually handled in a light and amusing style, and often deal with familiar incidents in everyday life. The reason for this policy is as follows:

The writer has always believed that fundamental Spiritual, Philosophical, and Metaphysical Truths could be stated in the plainest and simplest language, so that any intelligent child could understand them. It is true that most writings on these great subjects have been very obscure, and full of technical jargon; but the present writer believes that to be unnecessary.

Certain subjects, such as the higher mathematics, for instance, must remain out of reach of the layman; but this is not important because they do not concern his practical life. The understanding of Spiritual Truth, on the other hand, is not only the concern of Everyman, but is a vital need of his life; and it must necessarily therefore be possible for him to obtain it in a form which he can use. The loftiest and the most profound spiritual knowledge alike must be capable of being understood by any reasonably intelligent person over ten years of age.

These great Truths are actually revealed to us, not in the pages of inaccessible treatises, but in the seemingly petty and unimportant details of everyday life. Such practical details—the problems and experiences of day to day living—present the questions, and also furnish the answers to the great problems of human life, when one has the Spiritual Key.

The writer tries as far as possible to avoid the use of technical terminology, and never employs a word of three syllables where a word of two syllables will do.

Each of these Sparks illustrates one or more of the Laws of psychology or metaphysics. Try in each case to find out for yourself which is the particular Law involved, and then see if you are using that Law constructively in your own life. If you are not, you must change your habits of thinking without delay, for *the Laws of Thought are the Laws of Destiny.*

From Sparks of Truth

INDEX

233

234